To Amy —
Enjoy — and
Thanks for your
support!
Greg Mull

Amy — Please keep in
touch and we will
work together!
Love Cheri

The Red-Headed Cook of the Desert

Meth, Murder and Motherhood

Judy Muller
WITH CHERI MATHEWS

DEDICATIONS

To the parole board member who said "You should write a book"

To all those who overcome abuse and addiction despite overwhelming odds

To a friendship born from hours and hours of rigorous honesty, laughter, and more than a few tears

CONTENTS

Prologue

What Do You Think?

"*By the time I was in High School, the physical abuse was over. But the emotional abuse was worse and it lasted throughout Junior High and High School. Every day. Every day. Dad would come home from work, start drinking, and call me out. 'What do you think?' he would ask me, over and over. 'What do you want me to think?' I would ask. There were no right answers. He told me I was stupid and an idiot and he wanted me to think. 'WHAT DO YOU THINK?'*

I would start crying. And he would say, finally, 'You don't think, that's your fucking problem.' And then there were those times he would get really angry and say, 'You're going to be a whore just like your mother!'

One night, I finally stood up to him. 'What do I think? I think you're driving me crazy!'

And I got up and walked away.

—Cheri Mathews

Chapter 1

First Impressions

I met Cheri Mathews just before the pandemic closed down our little community in rural Colorado, in the Spring of 2020. Cheri was working as a waitress at *Kristi's Kitchen*, a favorite eatery attached to the local saloon, *The Lone Cone*. In Norwood, a town of about 600 people, any new face gets noticed. So I paid attention when my brother, who also lives here, said to me, "If you're looking for a good story, I think you should meet the new waitress at *Kristi's Kitchen*. She has a great personality, she's good at her job, and everyone really likes her. Also, she says she is on lifetime parole for murder."

I had never met anyone serving "lifetime parole," so I rose to the bait. I found myself at *Kristi's* for lunch soon after that, introducing myself to Cheri Mathews, the parolee in question. She was, indeed, a likeable, energetic, outgoing woman in her fifties, with a striking physical presence: tall and fit, with red hair and a winning smile. My brother had told her I might be interested in her story, and she didn't flinch at all from the prospect. Could we have lunch on her day off, I asked, perhaps in her nearby town of Nucla?

And so I found myself seated in a booth at Nucla's *Fifth Avenue Grill* (absolutely no similarity to any restaurant on the famous avenue of the same name), under the gaze of numerous antlered heads on the walls, my notebook and pen at the ready.

Unsure of where to begin, I went with the obvious: "Why don't you start by telling me about the murder?"

"Which one?" she replied.

And I was hooked.

So began a conversation that spanned several months and traveled down some very dark roads, weaving Cheri's recollections with those of her family and friends, adding up to an against-all-odds story of redemption. What follows is a pastiche of remembrances from different sources, but primarily from Cheri's own extensive prison writings and our many months of intimate conversations. One of her former bunkmates from prison responded to my request for a phone interview with a sentiment I would hear more than once: "I always expected I would get a call like this one day. I just knew someone would write her story."

AN EASY GUIDE TO READING OUR STORY

Because this narrative is a compilation of a variety of voices and memories, I offer this simple guide to understanding who is speaking at various times.

If the narrative is in bold typeface, it comes from conversations between Judy and Cheri, conversations that primarily occurred over the phone during the pandemic.

If the narrative is in italicized typeface, it comes directly from the extensive autobiography that Cheri wrote during her incarceration, from her English class essays in prison, or her other written remembrances and letters.

Chapter 2

No Thanks for the Memories

Cheri Shaw was born on Thanksgiving Day, 1960, in Northridge, California into somewhat thankless circumstances. Her parents, Robert Shaw and Carole Sue Lennon, married because of the pregnancy, and their brief time together was marked by violence, both verbal and physical. Cheri's entire childhood, until the age of 18, was spent in the San Fernando Valley, where – in the words of her childhood friend- "all those cities blend together," a vast landscape of wide streets, little shade, endless strip malls, imposing intersections, a numbing geometric sameness broken only by the interruption of cement flood control channels, where trash was more plentiful than water. Cheri's house, in Van Nuys, in the center of the Valley, was not all that far from the treelined streets of the upscale community of Encino, on the posh side of the 101 freeway. Not far, that is, when measured in miles, but a world away when measured in expectations and opportunities.

Cheri has, of course, no memories of her first few years living with her parents in Van Nuys. But she pieced together an account of the family history as it was related to her by her parents, and which she recounted in a lengthy biography (27 pages, single-spaced) that she wrote during her incarceration, decades later. We pick up that story in 1963, when Cheri was three.

While my mother was pregnant with my sister Susie, her brother came to stay with us. Uncle Ray, a big red-headed guy who I am told was very sweet to us, moved into my bedroom. I don't remember this, because I was very young, but my father told me that Ray left a goodbye note one day, saying he was going to Arizona where his estranged wife was living with her parents.

While in Arizona, Uncle Ray killed his wife and her parents, shot them to death. I learned about this years later. My father told me the police came to our house in Van Nuys to look for Ray, broke down the door and came into my room with guns at my head until they realized it was me in the bed and not Uncle Ray. Police eventually tracked him down. Ray was convicted and sentenced to life in the Arizona State Penitentiary.

It would not be the last encounter I would have with Uncle Ray. Or the police, for that matter.

This was the same year Kennedy was assassinated. It was also the year my mother left.

I was three and Susie was just a baby. Years later, Mom told me she left because she was abusing us, shaking us, and going into rages. It was for our own good, she said. My father never really got over it. He loved and hated her. He was obsessed with her. I looked like my Mom, so I would get that rage directed at me. He told me, over and over, for years, what a whore she was and that I would be like her.

My father hired a babysitter, Diane "Penny" Potter, to watch us during the day while he was working at the family's Chevron station. Penny was a topless dancer at a Canoga Park bar and she would take us there if she had to work a shift. We would help the bartender wash dishes, hiding behind the bar. When my Dad married Penny, she did her best to become a mother and a homemaker. Our home had to be meticulous, and we were given chores to do. But a neat home could not protect us from my Dad's moods. Penny tried to be our Mom, but she was codependent and he came first. Money was tight and Penny did her best with the allowance given to her by Dad. I remember her saving coupons, washing clothes at the laundromat, and shopping at thrift stores for our clothes. We always had everything we needed physically, just a little bit lacking in the healthy communication department.

Penny tried her best, but her best could be pretty rough. When I did something wrong, like walking home in the rain from elementary school, she spanked me with brushes, wooden spoons, and metal spatulas. Looking back, I believe she was acting out of fear. It scared her when she couldn't find me, and her fear would turn to anger.

When I was 12 years old, Penny caught me smoking at the park with an older girl. I had told the girl where I lived, because we planned to run away together. That night, she sneaked up to the side of my house, but she mistakenly looked through my parents' window, instead of mine. My dad jumped out of bed naked, grabbed his shotgun and hauled ass outside. Penny called the cops but the girl took off. Penny put two and two together pretty quick, and told me I was going to start looking like a 12-year-old instead of a teenager. So she cut my hair short and cut up my hip huggers and short tops. And she made me wear her old dresses to school, which I hated.

Once, she fed me horsemeat, even though she knew I loved horses. She told me what it was after I had eaten it. We were pretty poor back then, so maybe that's why she did it. But I cried and gagged until she let me go to my room without having to finish it.

But Dad was worse. When we were little, the abuse was physical. He scared us to death. If Susie or I walked in front of the TV while he was watching, he would kick us to get out of the way. We stayed in our room or outside. Not only was I afraid of Dad, but I didn't know what he wanted from me. I was basically a good kid. I got good grades, I helped around the house, and I loved our animals.

But I did have a problem: I was already developing addictive tendencies and I had zero impulse control. I was addicted to sugar and would steal as much brown sugar as I could get away with. I stole candy from the store and I would sneak into my parents' room while they were *sleeping to steal money from my dad's wallet. This would escalate into other addictions in later years.*

I also became an escape artist from reality. I used to retreat into my fantasy world, a desert island with just my dog and a herd of horses. I would figure out how to survive, with weapons to hunt and fish and I could just stay there forever. I "went there" all the time. When my Dad would pull up to the house in his truck, my stomach would go into knots. I'd be in my room and I would "go away." But at dinner, Susie and I had to walk past him in his chair to get to the kitchen. Susie and I would sit at a counter in the kitchen while Dad and Penny ate on TV trays in the living room. When I was in trouble, the anger would come off him like waves, and he would clench his jaw. I would never know when he would lash out. He would tell me he loved me after he beat me. He wasn't one for affection, but we had to kiss him goodnight every night.

I remember once when he caught me in a lie. He took me into the garage and he put my hand on a block and took the axe and acted like he was going to cut off my hand for lying to him.

This was in elementary school. I had written a note to one of the boys calling him a fucker, and my dad wanted me to confess to it. I lied all the way to the chopping block.

That was a bad day.

Judy: I know he didn't follow through on that threat, but the terror must have been visceral. When you talk about your childhood, I find myself wishing I could go back in time and rescue that girl, who simply had the misfortune of being born to a mother who abandoned her and an abusive father.

Cheri: Oh, no, no, no! I loved my father. Idolized him. Yes, he was emotionally challenged. But I always thought of him as that rock-hard man I idolized. He just had no parenting skills, no coping skills.

Cheri with her father, Robert Shaw, and sister Susie

Cheri's rationalization of her father's lack of "parenting skills" is inextricably linked to her unconscious sense of responsibility for the underdogs in life. Her automatic response to bullies is also deeply rooted in her protective attitude towards her younger sister, Susie. Because that sister has caused so much turmoil in the family over the years, Cheri's emotions are still somewhat mixed. Susie was not beaten and ridiculed in the same way Cheri was, but her life was pretty much a living hell from the get-go.

My sister Susie did not suffer the same kind of treatment. Her abuse took the form of neglect. I remember being lectured in the kitchen, while Susie was in the bedroom banging her head against the wall, over and over. She had serious behavior problems for as long as I can remember. She screamed and pulled her hair and scratched her face. She wet the bed until she was in her teens. They punished her for that. She was forced to sit in the front yard with wet sheets over her head. I had to bring her with me anywhere I went, and if I tried to leave without her, she would scream and cry until I went back for her. This stunt saved my ass one day. We always took the alleyway to the elementary school and one morning I walked ahead of her. Susie threw herself down in the usual fashion, but I wasn't giving in so easy. I figured I would walk to the end of the alley before I would go back for her. A pickup truck drove up and stopped suddenly. A man jumped out of the driver's side, his dick out of his pants, and grabbed me. Susie let out a scream and stopped him in his tracks. Once he saw her, he jumped in the truck and took off. But before we could get out of there, the son of a bitch flipped a U-turn and was coming back at us. I pushed Susie into a car port and was ready to jump a fence, but the dude kept going. We ran to school and told a teacher, who called the police. I don't think my dad ever got over that. He became obsessed with teaching me how to defend myself. That was in junior high.

When I got older, in my teens, I was too big to physically punish. So the emotional abuse got much, much worse. After Dad would drink in the evening, he would launch into his "What do you THINK?" attacks. Even though I knew where it was headed, with him concluding that I would end up a whore, like my mother, I was expected to sit there and take it. He would go on and on about her, never mind that Penny was hearing all this. She would try to intervene, but he would tell her to stay out of it because she wasn't my mother.

On the flip side of those interrogations, he would lecture me on "the code":

- Never be a coward
- Never be a snitch
- Never back down and run away, because if you run, they will come after you and kill you
- Never point a gun and not use it
- Never shoot someone and not finish it

Sometimes he would teach me how to kill people, if I had to, including how to crush the larynx and use the heel of my hand to drive the nose cartilage into the brain, how to bite and take off the nose or rip the throat, how to use a knife so your attacker can't take it away, and how to put my fingers through eye sockets and drive them into the brain.

This started in junior high school. I would just sit there and disassociate. I don't think I took it outside our home, because keeping family business private was another part of the code. My friends all loved my Dad, because they never saw that side of him.

Christina Karlen was one of those friends. She agreed to speak with me on the phone about those days when she and Cheri were close pals.

"I envied her family life, because I didn't know about all the punishment. I just knew she lived in an immaculate home, and she had chores and responsibilities. She was grounded for a whole summer because she was caught kissing a boy. I thought that was harsh, but I also wished my parents had given me more punishments, showing they cared. I thought her Dad was cool. He was good-looking and fun. The summer that "Jaws" came out, we talked about how the part played by the actor Robert Shaw was like her father, who had the same name. She talked about her Dad with a tone of hero-worship. Years later, after we reconnected and I learned about her scary life, I thought, 'How could this happen? She was in honors classes, MVP on the swim team, the smartest person I knew.'"

Chapter 3

Swimming Upstream

Cheri's school years were tumultuous. She attended four junior high schools, getting suspended repeatedly for smoking or fighting. And yet, she was an "A" student.

Judy: How in the world did you manage to maintain an "A" average?

Cheri: I crammed. I have gotten away with it all my life. Even the drug and alcohol counseling classes in prison. I was named Salutatorian. But I had trouble with my memory, lots of problems. I would forget what I learned in about a month. 'Use it or lose it' fit me to a T.

A lot of my anger from home followed me to school, and I fought a lot. I had a hero complex, and I hated bullies. So when I saw someone getting bullied, I stepped in to defend them. I had bad acne at that time, which made me feel ugly, different, ashamed. I had muscles, so I wore long sleeves to hide my arms. The truth of it was, I became the bully when I fought the bullies. After getting kicked out of public schools, I had to go to a Baptist school, which was tough. I mean, my dad claimed to be an atheist and my favorite singer was Alice Cooper. But I was on the softball team, and I was a really good player. My coach was also my Bible teacher. He was very prejudiced against Adventists,

Mormons and Jehovah's Witnesses. At the time, Penny was meeting with Jehovah's Witnesses in the afternoons at our house. I don't remember if my dad knew or not. So when I wrote essays for my bible class, I just copied articles from Penny's collection of Jehovah's Witness Watchtower pamphlets. The teacher never caught on, and always gave me A's.

Judy: So you were getting good grades there, doing well on the softball team. What went wrong? Why did you leave?

Cheri: My Dad got involved.

My coach was going to take me to the athletic awards ceremony, but when my Dad heard that, he flipped out, accusing me of wanting to hook up with a guy the coach knew. One day after practice, Dad showed up at school and piled the team into his pickup to take everyone to the Pizza Parlor. Dad was drunk and while we were there, he punched my Bible teacher.

Next day, I'm in Bible class and the teacher has a black eye. And he says, "We're going to pray for Cheri's Dad."

I said, "Fuck you. And by the way, all my essays came from Watchtower pamphlets."

So I got sent to the principal's office. He gave me a choice: suspension or swats. I chose the swats, which were delivered with a sawed-off oar. He hit me so hard I slammed into the wall, harder than I had ever been hit at home.

"FUCK YOU," I screamed. And so I was suspended anyway.

I was afraid to go home, so I talked my best friend into running away from home. We ended up in a garden center where they grow trees and tried to sleep there. It was scary, so we called home. My first day back at school, someone told on me for smoking in the bathroom and I was expelled.

I was 12 years old.

I was allowed to go back to one of the junior high schools, Mulholland, where I had been suspended for fighting before. But only on the condition that I would agree to counseling. That didn't have much of an impact, since part of our family "code" was that when you left the house, you didn't talk about the family business. I defended my Dad, no matter what.

Cheri's best friend- Christina Karlen (nee Olmstead)- went to a different school, but they bonded over shared adventures, which began in the 4th grade. Cheri remembers it vividly. But then, Cheri remembers almost everything vividly, which is somewhat astonishing, given the never-ending turmoil of her life, including years of drug abuse.

Christina was literally in the gutter when I met her. One of those tunnels near a flood control channel. I said, "How did you get down there?" She guided me down there – and we made a plan to return with flashlights. We learned that if we crawled on our bellies, we could get to a storm drain that led to the aqueduct and the L.A. River. There was some pretty greenery around it and that's where we would hang out.

Christina: Cheri always had the courage to see an idea through to completion. You know that bridge that crosses White Oak and Victory? We were out there with our dogs and another girl, who agreed to watch the dogs while we tried to climb under the bridge. I was the acrobat, the gymnast, so I figured out how to do it. We climbed up the side wall of the aqueduct, grabbed the support beams to swing over the middle, under the bridge. The flood channel was far below us. We got to the big cement center support in the middle, which stopped us. So we turned around to go back, only to realize that the beams were now on our left, and it was too awkward to get hold of them and swing back. Our friend, below the bridge with the dogs, called the fire department. When they showed up, they drove their truck down into the aqueduct to put up a ladder to rescue us. By that time, a huge crowd had gathered on the bridge, along with the police.

We jumped down to the ladder, which made them mad. We were supposed to wait for the firefighters to reach us. The police arrested us, took us to the station and handcuffed us to a bench. Handcuffs! We were 12 years old! They called our parents.

Penny was the first to arrive. We could see her big pregnant belly in the video camera at the station entrance. Penny had had 6 miscarriages and was supposed to be on bedrest, so she wasn't too happy about having to come get me. But I didn't get into any trouble, because my Dad thought that anything that I did that showed bravery was fine.

Christina: My mom was very angry and very vocal. Cheri said, "It's not like we were arrested or anything." My mom said, "You WERE arrested!"

Now that I look back on it, I can see that Cheri was very good at shooting herself in the foot. She refused to wear her dress at the right length at that Baptist school, bucking authority. And these encounters would become monumental things. Although I didn't do alcohol, we were all experimenting with drugs in high school.

I started smoking cigarettes and pot when I was twelve. Later that turned into alcohol, downers, Quaaludes, reds, acid (my favorite). There were plenty of drugs available in the 70's. I wanted to fit in. I felt more powerful, pretty, and suddenly had friends. I found an escape from my home life. On weekends, when I was supposed to be at a football game, I was getting drunk or high. I never made it to one football game in high school.

Christina: Despite that rebellious side, Cheri was the epitome of doing a good job simply for the sake of doing a good job. She got A's, was really smart and so brave. One night, I remember, I was spending the night at her house and we heard noises in the back yard that scared us. I was ready to climb under the bed. But she grabbed a coat hanger out of the closet and stormed outside. That impressed the hell out of me. Most impressive, maybe, is when she joined the local swim team because I had joined it.

Judy: Why was that impressive?

Christina: Cheri couldn't swim.

Cheri: I told the swim coach I couldn't swim, but I wanted to learn. By my senior year, I spent a lot of time at the pool, working on my backstroke and freestyle. I won two firsts in the L.A. city finals in both the 10th and 11th grades. In my senior year, I took two firsts and one second in the city varsity finals. But I missed being swimmer of the year in the city-wide championships by 1/10th of a second. My uncle Chris came down from the stands and said, "What was THAT?" I never raced again. I saw it as a failure. My swim coach was disappointed because the Air Force Academy had been interested in giving me a scholarship.

Judy: You gave up the chance for a scholarship at the Air Force Academy? And a career as an officer?

Cheri: No one ever talked about "careers" in my house. My dad told me if I wanted to go to college, I was ass-out of luck because he wasn't going to support that. He told me I was out of the house when I turned 18. So I joined the Army, and 4 days after my 18th birthday, I was gone. Out of that house for the first time in my life. I went into the Army and Christine joined the circus as a trapeze artist, a "flyer." She married her "catcher." They had two boys and traveled the world. We lost touch for a long time.

Christina: Years later, after I divorced and left the circus, I was living in the small town of Cuyama, and Cheri came looking for me. I broke down in tears when I saw her, because I had completely lost track of her. She invited me and my kids to visit her place in the high desert, an area so remote the streets have no names. If you want to stay on a road, straight is not the way to go. You've got to know where to turn. We got lost, but after some time passed, a man in a fancy Cadillac, with a driver, came to pick us up and take us to

Cheri's double-wide. It was immaculate, just like her house had been. Her friends were kind, but weird. She called them her "associates." At one point, she asked me to get something from her purse, and I saw a gun in there. And then, after we had starting talking and filling in the lost gaps in our lives, she shared the story of how she had killed a guy in self-defense. We were both crying, but I knew at that moment that I could never bring my kids there again. So we lost connection. For a long, long time.

Cheri: I told Chris about killing Frank Belize. She didn't want to know me after that.

Christina: She was tough. Courageous. Great athlete. Got top grades. But she self-sabotaged a lot. She worried constantly about turning out like her mother.

From a letter written from Cheri to her daughter, Michelle, and son, Jason, in June 1999, from prison in California:

Grandma writes me about once a week and she told me about you falling off the [swim meet] starting block, Michelle. My last year in high school, I was at the L.A. City Swim Finals and I was racing the 50-free. I froze on the block and watched everyone else dive in. I caught up but still lost the race and came in 2nd. I quit swimming. See how different you are from me. Both of you are fighters and I love it in you. Don't ever, ever give up your dreams and you will achieve them! I love you both so much!
Mom

Chapter 4

Never Be A Snitch: Living The Code

Judy: Cheri, how did you feel about your mom, given the fact that she left you and your sister with your Dad when you were so young, and never came back?

Cheri: She told me she didn't have a choice, that she was suffering from depression and had been physically abusive to us. And I loved visiting her. She married a horse trainer and lived on a ranch in Chula Vista. She had a horse that never lost a race. Over the years, she became a talented horse trainer and jockey herself. She divorced and remarried a lot.

Ron Mori, Carole's fourth husband and Cheri's stepfather, agreed to talk with me about Carole's role as a mother, and as a woman who seemed to be a magnet for men. She married 6 times.

Ron: Carole was beautiful and talented. Everything she did, she was good at it. Her nickname was "Rowdy Red" at the racetrack where she worked as an exercise rider. But she was manic, bipolar, and every day was a roller coaster ride. We had a son together, Ronnie, and I raised her son Kevin from her second marriage, as well as Susie [Cheri's younger sister], who came to live with us when her father and Penny said they couldn't handle her anymore. Susie was the death of our marriage, in trouble all the time, getting our kids to take drugs. Carole and I drank too much and fought all the time. We divorced in 1985.

Judy: When did you first meet Cheri?

Ron: Her high school graduation in Van Nuys. That's when we brought Susie back to live with us in Fallon, Nevada. Susie was 14. Cheri went into the Army, but I got to know her when she would visit us. I love Cheri. She is a straight shooter. She never snitched or squealed on anybody.

Judy: That seems like an odd thing to mention.

She never snitched. She had a sense of honor, and loyalty.

Judy: What kind of a mother was Carole to Cheri and Susie?

Carole never talked to me about abandoning the girls, but she stood up for them, right or wrong. And that was a problem. Carole felt guilty, so she wouldn't discipline them.

Cheri: *I loved visiting her. It was like a dream. Susie and I got to go to the race track, experience ranch life, ride horses. She spoiled us, because she didn't have to deal with us all the time. She did show some remorse for leaving us. But her life was chaos. She took speed to keep her weight down for racing, and she introduced me to "bennies." I was 12 at the time.*

One day during our summer of talks, Cheri and I decided to meet in person, pre-vaccine, socially distanced to the degree that was possible, because she wanted to share photos of her friends and family, an increasingly complex cast of characters, at least to me.

The photo album was one of the few possessions left to her after she got paroled from prison. Tucked inside a pocket, I found an article from a magazine, *Nevada Horse Life*, entitled "Fallon's Female Jockey," featuring Cheri's mother:

"Working in her garden, with auburn braids hanging from beneath a sun hat, Carole Mori looks like an ad from a home-maker's magazine. This 34 year-old mother of four with the winning

smile does not fit the image of a person who could handle a fractious thoroughbred on a race track. But she can – with confidence and ease."

Accompanying this article are several photos of Carole Mori with her favorite mount, "Tempest Tempo," dressed in riding clothes and helmet, grinning broadly.

She is the spitting image of her daughter, Cheri.

Years later, in 1998, the year Cheri started serving a 16 to life term in prison – Carole was featured in another magazine, *Petworld*, in an article entitled "The Tiger Touch, Exotic Feline Sanctuary." In these photos, she is posing with various big cats – rescued and cared for in a preserve in Nevada, where she worked as a trainer. Her favorites were Detonator, a male Bengal tiger, Rocky, an African male lion, and Peggy Sue, a Siberian Lynx. Carole is reclining with them in the photos, smiling somewhat provocatively.

She still looks exactly like Cheri.

Cheri's mom, Carole,
with one of her favorite big cats at "Tiger Touch" reserve

Carole was certainly much more complicated than that magazine description of a "34 year-old mother of four with a winning smile." She would go on to become an equally complicated grandmother. I asked Michelle Mathews Dyer, her granddaughter, about that in a recent interview.

"My grandma was bipolar, so everything was always extreme. Of course, as a kid, I didn't know she was bipolar. I just thought she was tough and interesting. I remember when I was in school in Fallon, Nevada, my class went on a field trip to Tiger Touch, the reserve where Grandma worked. I have a picture of me with the lion. I remember walking the baby tiger on a leash."

[Long pause]

"A lot of my childhood I have blocked out."

Cheri, on the other hand, remembers almost every detail of her childhood, especially this one:

One visit had a huge impact on my life. When I was 12, Susie and I went to visit my Mom in Hemet, California where she and husband #3, Kevin Lee Stucki, managed a thoroughbred breeding farm for the cosmetics magnate, Max Factor. This was in the early 70's, and my mother had just had a double mastectomy, was in a lot of pain and on meds. She was also depressed. While I was there, a man she called Bruce, "a friend from Texas," came to visit and he babysat us sometimes. One day when Mom was away from the house, the cops showed up at the ranch, and "Bruce" hid in a closet. The police were looking for a man fitting his description. I lied and told them there was no one like that around, and they left.

"Bruce" would entertain us with tales of pranks he pulled. He told me that he and "K.L." had sneaked onto Cal Worthington's Ranch. Worthington owned a big car dealership and in his commercials, he would bring out a tiger or elephant or some other animal. Well, "Bruce" and "K.L." trailered the baby elephant and took it bar hopping. I thought that was hilarious.

Later, I learned that "Bruce from Texas" was actually my Uncle Ray, Mom's brother, the same Uncle Ray who was serving a life sentence for a triple murder. He had escaped from Arizona State Penitentiary, taken a family hostage and made them drive him to California, where he was hiding out with Mom. The police caught him later, but I didn't know about any of this. My mom went into a deep depression and cried the rest of the time we were there. She didn't get into trouble because Ray was not on the ranch when the police caught up with him. When we asked where our visitor had gone, Mom said, simply, "Bruce had to go back to Texas."

When we returned to our house in Van Nuys, all hell broke loose. My grandmother Helen and step-grandfather Poppy had driven us home. My dad hated Helen and she hated him. They started fighting and it came out about Ray. When my grandparents left, my dad yelled for me to come out of my bedroom. He and Penny were both drinking. My dad asked me about Ray, and I told him I didn't know anyone called Ray. My dad beat me all over the house, and kept calling me a liar.

It was one of the worst beatings of my life.

I didn't understand what was happening, but I honestly thought I would die. Even Penny wouldn't help me. She was drunk and angry, which was so unusual. After they figured out I wasn't lying, they started firing questions at me, until they realized this visitor I called Bruce was actually Ray.

That's when the shitstorm really got bad. I broke down and cried. I spilled my guts. I told them Mom had given me speed.

I betrayed her.

Here are the details I remember. Penny had given us beef stroganoff for dinner, and when Dad said he was going to call the police to report Mom for harboring a fugitive, I threw my plate of food at him, screaming at him to leave Mom alone, because she was sick.

It was the first time I had ever really stood up to him.

My dad called my mom instead of the police, and I could hear them screaming at each other on the phone.

Then he gave the phone to me. And Mom told me I was a fucking snitch and she hated my guts. I never heard from her again until she showed up at my high school graduation five years later with husband #4 (Ron Mori) and a new brother (Ronnie).

I never snitched on anyone again. The shame I felt was intense.

My uncle went back to prison, where he died in 1998.

Coincidentally, that was also the year I was sentenced to life in prison.

Chapter 5

My Better Angels

Cheri remembers three prominent people from her youth, three people who represented something pure and honorable, bright lights in her often dark world.

My grandpa Robert Shaw was gruff and a great cook. He and my grandma Hazel helped raise us when Mom left, until Hazel died of cancer when I was five years old. He had a cabin near Lake Isabella and I remember him showing me how to fly fish. We always had holiday dinners at his house, but Dad would get drunk and it usually ended in a fight. My grandpa was always in my life. I loved him dearly, but something happened years later and it wrecked me. I had left my husband Jerry because the abuse had become worse. My grandpa made a lunch date with me at a restaurant. He never had done that, and he never did it again. He told me that day that was I was to go back to my husband because I'd made my bed and now I had to lie in it and make it work. He didn't care that Jerry hit me. I couldn't believe that my grandfather was telling me this and I felt betrayed. I did go back to Jerry, but I never felt the trust for my grandfather that I used to.

My uncle Chris Shaw was my hero. He was handsome and athletic, a fireman. He took Susie and me camping and taught us how to water ski. He did the things my dad didn't. He tried his best to fill that void.

But he had high expectations of me that could be unreasonable sometimes. We used to go water skiing on the Colorado River near Parker Dam. One of his fireman buddies had a place on the river. Uncle Chris and I were out in the boat and I jumped in with my skis. The boat died, and I was being pulled down the river by current. Chris called out to me to swim for shore. I was about 10 years old, floating down the middle of the river, and the dam was getting closer. I was scared of being sucked down and swam towards shore as hard as I could. I made it to a trailer park next to the dam, over a mile away from where I started. No one came for me, so with skis in tow, barefoot, wearing my bikini and life vest, I walked down a dirt road in the 100 degree heat until I made it back. By that time, Chris had fixed the boat and taken other people skiing. I was pissed, and my feet hurt. He just smiled at me and said, "You're tough and you made it back just fine. I knew you could do it."

After my dad died and I got divorced, my alcoholism was so bad Uncle Chris couldn't take it. I showed up at his fire station drunk and he told me he refused to watch me die like he watched my dad die. I was pretty much disowned and I was too hurt by the rejection to understand until later that he did the only thing he could to protect himself. He had healthy boundaries and I never knew what those were. I did see him again during my last years in prison. He came to visit but it was awkward. He had found religion and I had rejected mine.

He did make copies of family pictures for me which I really appreciated, since mine were lost.

The other significant person is [my baby sister] Mandy. She was born when I was 15. As far as I was concerned, the sun rose and set on her. Penny had 7 miscarriages so she had to stay in bed throughout the pregnancy to come to full term. I helped with the house and cooking and with Mandy after she was born. Penny protected her fiercely. She *told my dad that Mandy would not end up like me and that he was not to discipline her.*

In a phone interview with Mandy, I asked her about her interaction with her dad, Bob Shaw, who died when she was 8. "The only time he ever grabbed me to scold me," she said, "was when I was running around the coffee table. He grabbed me by the arm and was knocking me on my forehead with his knuckles, saying 'This is what it will feel like when you fall and hit that table!' My Mom came out of the kitchen and yelled, 'And THIS is what that feels like to HER!' And she hauled off and hit him. Broke his nose. He never touched me after that."

Mandy did turn out okay. She was eight when Dad died and 14 when Penny died in a car accident. Today, she has two beautiful daughters and lives in Ohio. She used to write, but she doesn't anymore.
So I leave her to her life.

Judy: When you wrote those words in prison, did you have any hope that you might resurrect the relationship with Mandy?

Cheri: Yes, and today we are in touch, writing and talking. She is incredibly important to me. But when I was out there, before I went away, I wanted to stay away from them, because they didn't deserve to be around me. I was criminally minded. Even though I had a moral compass when it came to empathy for others, I was addicted to the rush of doing bad things. Stealing from my parents, or climbing a bridge, or selling drugs or cooking drugs. It made me feel alive. I was hooked on danger from a young age. It was a rush to survive these situations.

Judy: You mentioned another good memory in your prison biography– a summer working in the mountains when you were 16 years old.

I had been accepted, along with my friend Tammi Schoenfield, to participate in the Youth Conservation Corps. It was amazing that my dad let me go! We lived in Kings Canyon for the summer, working and backpacking. I lost my virginity that summer to one of the forest rangers.

It wasn't a romantic memory.

But there was a memory from that summer that had a profound impact on me. I was walking to the community bathroom one day with Tammi's mom, when she suddenly spun on a dime and took off running. At first, I didn't understand why. Then I saw it. A large black bear growling at me. I froze. There was no one around me. I could hear people yelling, but not what they were saying, because the blood was rushing to my head. I started to move when it looked like he was turning away, but as soon as I did that, he spun around, lowered his head, opened his mouth and charged me. Everything went into slow motion. My knees were actually knocking together, and an image of Olive Oyl from the Popeye cartoon popped into my head, with her long legs wobbling together. And I prayed that the bear would take my head so I wouldn't have to watch.

At the last moment, I went completely calm and screamed "Fuck you!" in his face as loud as I could. He sideswiped me and took off. They eventually caught him and released him in the high country.

I was traumatized pretty badly. Scared to death of bears after that.

But I was also aware that dying was no big deal. I knew I could be brave in the worst moment. I could turn fear into anger and survive the worst moments.

Judy: When I first read this passage from your prison autobiography, I was struck by the short shrift you gave to the way you lost your virginity. What in the world was an adult forest ranger doing seducing a teenage girl working at the camp? Not a "romantic memory," you said, but nothing more.

Cheri: He was actually very young, and it was consensual. But it hurt and I wanted it to stop. I never talked to him again.

Judy: Any romance at all in your adolescence?

Cheri: I was never a romantic. Not soft or affectionate. I was hardcore. And I had a terrible body image.

I had a couple of short term boyfriends in high school, and some sexual encounters my senior year. I believed I was about the ugliest person around. Some of my "friends" helped me believe that. They gave me a party when I was leaving for the army, where a few of them suggested I was enlisting because I was a lesbian and so manly looking. A couple of my high school friends were just "mean girls." I ended up fighting the girl who threw the party. I hit her one time and knocked her down.

I left crying.

Chapter 6

You're in the Army Now (Except When You're Not)

Within four months of joining the U.S. Army in 1978, Cheri was AWOL on two separate occasions. And yet, by the end of her Army stint in 1981, she'd been promoted to E-4, and was honorably discharged. With a good conduct medal, no less. She had earned various decorations and citations, as well, including the NCO Professional Development Ribbon, Marksman (M-16 rifle), Expert (Hand Grenade) and Sharpshooter (.38 Caliber Pistol).

She also got married. It lasted about three months.

Cheri: I met Tim Krueger when I was at Ft. Riley, in Kansas. We were living in the same barracks and he was dealing drugs. He proposed with a ring and everything.

Judy: And that's all it took?

Cheri: All I remember thinking was, "Somebody actually wants to marry me." So I brought him back to L.A. for a church wedding, so that all my "friends" could see I was not gay.

Judy: Did you love him?

Cheri: I wasn't capable of knowing what love is. He was alcoholic and extremely jealous. He ripped up old photos of my past boyfriends, got drunk and wrecked my new pickup truck. I told him

to get out. He cleaned out my bank account. I got a formal divorce later, when I got out of the Army, but my name was now Cheri Lee Kreuger, not Cheri Lee Shaw.

Judy: By the time your Army service is over, two years out of high school, you've left behind a trail of contradictory behavior. Sometimes you receive praise and accolades for your service, and other times you are facing disciplinary action that's quite serious. It's hard to follow, much less fathom.

Cheri: I sometimes see myself as a pinball in a pinball machine. Never stopping to think of consequences. Just do what's in front of me, ignore consequences, rinse and repeat. Mindless.

Judy: And yet, you told me that you really liked the Army.

Cheri: I was really good at the Army. I aced basic training. I was placed in an experimental battalion, with men and women together for the first time. I loved the physical training, being treated the same as the men. I was a strong girl and was used to working out for hours in a pool. I went to Military Police school at Ft. McClellan, Alabama, because I knew that was a prerequisite for being accepted into the Canine Corps. And that was my goal. I wanted to work with dogs. But I was turned down when I applied, and it was like the rug being pulled out from under me.

Judy: Could you have re-applied later?

Cheri: Yes. But I did not have good coping skills and didn't have the frame of mind to understand that I could try again.

Judy: Reminds me of that swim meet. One setback and you were done.

Cheri: They were going to send me to Ft. Carson, Colorado for MP duty. But my only thought was that I could never be a "cop." I couldn't bust people for doing the same things I was doing. Drugs and alcohol were a part of my life. They made it easier to express myself. It never occurred to me to get sober, much less stay sober.

So, I went AWOL and headed for Tennessee.

Judy: Why Tennessee?

Cheri: I was headed to a friend's family home in Kingsport. A girl in my unit. She had asked me to spend Christmas break there and I couldn't afford to go back to L.A. I was only 18 years old, but I had beefed up to 200 pounds in the Army, partly because I no longer had Penny telling me what I could and couldn't eat. She always kept me on a very strict diet. I was bigger now, but I was also very strong.

Cheri decided to hitchhike to Tennessee on a cold, rainy day.

A guy pulled over and offered me a ride. He had a new Camaro and he was a good-looking guy. He's a clean-cut guy in a new car and I'm thinking I'm okay. Then he turned off the main highway and headed down a road into the deep woods. I froze. I knew I was in trouble, but I just sat there and didn't say anything. He stopped at some railroad tracks. Nothing but woods around us. He stopped the car and told me if I gave him a blow job, he would take me to the town of Gadsen.

I said, "Thanks, but no thanks," and got out of the car and started walking down the road. My clothes were still in his car but I didn't ask for them. He got out and started following me. He had a knife. I heard him call out, "You know I'm going to have to kill you when I'm done." My first thought was that my mom and dad were going to look for me, but no one would ever find me. I couldn't run, the blood was pumping in my head and I felt numb. He started running and I heard him right behind me. I spun around to face him. I vowed I would die before I would let him rape me. I got very calm and told him I was going to take the knife from him and kill him. Actually, I told him I would cut off his dick and he would die choking on it and I was going to bury him so no one would ever find him. And then I added, for good measure, thanks for the new car.

He started to back up, turned and ran, and jumped into the car.

Then I sort of woke up and the fear overwhelmed me. I still thought I was going to die. That he would come after me.

I ran and ran. It was pouring rain and I kept slipping down hills in the mud. I ripped the inside of my pants wide open because I was too fat for them. I just kept running.

Finally, I came to a group of houses. I chose a house with Hot Wheels and toys in the front yard, and knocked on the door. It was about 1 or 2 a.m.

A man and his wife opened the door and I said, "This might sound stupid, but do you please have a needle and thread?" Then I started to cry. They brought me inside and let me take a shower while the woman washed and sewed my pants. I told them what had happened, but they didn't call the police because I told them I was AWOL from the Army. They woke up their kids, and the whole family drove me to a truck stop. They bought me coffee and found a truckdriver who was willing to take me to Kingsport. The husband lied and said I was his sister and needed a ride to reach our sick mother. So I made it there safely.

Judy: Sounds like you faced down another wild animal, a more dangerous one, and you basically pulled off another "fuck you" defense strategy. You must have terrified the guy. And you certainly lucked out by knocking on the right door. So what happened when you got to Kingsport?

Cheri: I met up with a guy I had met earlier when I had spent Christmas there. His name was Robin and he was a moonshine runner. He had that twangy, backwoods southern accent and I really liked him. I guess it's fair to say that I didn't know what a red flag was back then. His mother was a horrible drunk and she and I got into a knock-down, drag-out fight in their apartment parking lot. She was screaming at Robin to "get that horrible whore off my car." The cops showed up and took me to jail on assault charges. In the courtroom, I felt like I was in a movie. They wanted to send me to a work camp for a year, but I kept saying, "Look, guys, I belong to the U.S. Army." After Robin's mom sobered up, she dropped the charges and I was released.

Judy: And you returned to your base in Alabama?

Cheri: I hitchhiked back and turned myself in. I had been gone a week. But it had been a terrifying week.

The one thing that tormented me over the years was that I had let a rapist get away to rape and maybe kill other girls. I had never gotten the license number and I never even told the Army what happened.

I went before the disciplinary committee and I told them I couldn't be a cop and that I wanted out of the Army. They said, "Too bad." I was confined to quarters (CTQ) and was scheduled to get an Article 15.

An Article 15 is more severe than a letter of reprimand and less severe than a court martial. The punishments can include reduction in rank, forfeitures, 60 days restriction, 45 days extra duty, or 30 days correctional custody.

Cheri didn't wait around long enough to find out which precise punishment she would be getting.

I rebelled. I started drinking a lot. I would break my confinement and go to the bar and get drunk and fight. They threw me in the brig a couple of times and my Lieutenant would come get me out. So I went AWOL again, this time with my friend Kathy and a couple of guys. We all went to Lancaster, Ohio, in a car the guys rented, to stay at Kathy's family farm. We told them we were all on leave. But it fell apart.

Judy: How so?
Cheri: The car rental place told the guys that if they did not return the car, they would be charged with grand theft. They had just rented it for a day and we'd been gone for more than a week.

The guys turned in the car and themselves. Kathy and I hitchhiked back later.

Because I had never received the Article 15 for the original AWOL, I was pending a punishment. So the second AWOL was considered desertion. I was thrown in the brig.

Judy: So now your situation is much, much more serious.

Cheri: I thought I was going to go to Leavenworth, going to prison. I was only 18 years old.

Judy: What saved you?

Cheri: I guess someone there thought I was worth another chance. They reduced the charges. I received a field grade Article 15, was kicked out of the MPs, and sent to truck driving school in Fort Dix, New Jersey.

After completing that training, I was sent to Fort Riley, Kansas, assigned to supply and transport. I went through bus driving school and was assigned to going into town to pick up new troops at the bus station or airport and drive them to their new units.

I had been in the Army for four months.

Judy: I have to say, you are the queen of second chances. How did the "do-over" go?

Cheri: I got into some more trouble when a bunch of soldiers I was supposed to drive to the base started harassing me, sexually harassing me. Then they locked me out of my bus. Their sergeant intervened, and stood next to me as I drove the bus, glaring at these guys in the seats. He was holding on tight to a pole and said, "Shake 'em up, Cheri."

So I did, driving like a maniac, with these guys getting tossed all over the place.

I guess I took it too far. There was a sergeant driving an officer's car behind me. When I stopped, he took down my name and unit. The next day, I was called into battalion headquarters and I figured I was going to be punished.

I was ushered into the office of Sergeant Major Eugene Stevens. He asked, "Were you the one driving like a crazy person on my post?" I said yes and he just grinned at me. "How would you like to be my new driver?"

Cheri's admiration for Stevens was so intense that she wrote about him for an English class in prison, many years later. Entitled

"My Rock," the essay began with a description of his voice when addressing soldiers in the First Infantry Division at Fort Riley.

"Hey JACKASS!" snarled the used-to-being-obeyed-right- fucking-now command.

The prevailing consensus was that he was hands-down the meanest, scariest SOB to be assigned to the post since General George Patton.

Her physical description of Stevens was etched in her memory, despite the passing years.

Deceptively small, his compact 5'10" 185 pound frame was every inch the mean, green, fighting machine, and woe to the traitorous grunt displaying any form of disrespect against duty, God, or country.... Perfectly shaved and cropped Marine-style flat top framed the head jutting out on a thick, muscled neck....Black, horn-rimmed government-issued glasses suspended above his flared nostrils magnifying the impassive slate-gray eyes that pinned down his opponent like a bug under a microscope....Camel cigarette jammed in between his teeth, he barked out the orders that kept the commanders of six different battalions jumping through his proverbial hoops until the mission of organizing troop movement and field exercises met his standard of excellence. Luckily, I had the opportunity to glimpse a lighter side.

Cheri's description of this relationship evokes a buried longing for a tough, but loving father figure, even if she would not have expressed it that way at the time. Or perhaps even now.

On rare occasions when the Sergeant Major and I were alone, he attentively listened to the dreams, fears, and questions of a naïve 18-year-old. Offering insightful wit, wisdom and unconditional friendship, he generously omitted the condescending smirks or judgments of someone much older and wiser. These opportunities usually took place during night training exercises atop some hill, sitting in the open Jeep overlooking mock war games being played out below. After sipping an ample amount of Jack Daniels, the military façade faded.

This hard-core military "rock" would soften, she says, on these occasions, and the Sgt. Major would share his pride in the wife "who had kept the home fires burning" while he was away on duty and regrets of missing so much of his son's life, the son who was then graduating college.

Spiritually shackled to his sense of duty, he surrendered to the loneliness of choices made long ago, with a vulnerability that taught me the true meaning of courage. I am forever grateful for the fond memories of an authentic warrior, imperfect role model, and trusted friend who taught me to see the intricate artistry within myself and others. The world erects a multitude of facades; it is up to me to remember that treasures may lie under the surface, even the surface of a rock.

Cheri: Eventually, the brigade commander, Colonel Guy P. Bowen, requested me as a driver and I stayed with him until I was discharged from the Army. He traveled to Germany, so I got to do and see a lot. I loved Europe.

But it was Sergeant Major Stevens who first saw something in me I didn't see in myself.

Judy: I would argue that he wasn't the first. Or the last. What's consistent throughout your story is your failure to see yourself as others did. From your grade school pal to your swim coach to your commanding officer, you had a steady stream of people telling you how smart, how accomplished, how strong you are. And yet.

Cheri: If I had my chances over again, my life would be totally different. My dad never thought I was smart enough to go to college. He wanted me to work at his gas station. He was proud, though, when I went into the military. He just never knew about the bad stuff. He knew I drove for a Colonel overseas, and that I made it to E4. Got a good conduct medal, of all things.

I wish I had re-enlisted.

But instead, I fell in love. This was in 1980. I was stationed at Ft. Riley, Kansas and I met Jerry Mathews in a bar. The Rock Quarry in Junction City, Kansas. He was gorgeous, really built, had a great smile.

The year before Cheri met the man who would become her second husband, she had another narrow escape. She mentioned it as an afterthought, perhaps because she had already survived so many dramatic attacks, both physical and emotional: an angry bear, a homicidal rapist, not to mention all the abuse she had suffered as a child, which would prove to be her most difficult and stubborn enemy.

But this particular incident seems so symbolic of her life of narrow escapes and second chances that I am including it here.

In 1979, when Cheri was leaving Ft. Dix for a new post at Ft. Riley, she secured two weeks leave so that she could travel to L.A., pick up her car and drive back to Kansas. Cheri and a girlfriend planned to buy tickets for American Airlines flight 191 from Chicago to L.A., and Cheri had let her parents know she would be on that plane. But a man who overheard them planning their trip interrupted them and said he was looking for someone to drive his car to L.A. "Perfect!" they thought. "We'll save the air fare and get a free road trip, too!" So instead of buying those tickets and getting aboard flight 191, they checked into a local motel, with plans to meet the guy the next day. Then they turned on the television news. The top story was a plane crash. Everyone aboard American Airlines flight 191 had been killed when the plane lost one engine after take-off, stalled, rolled to the left and plummeted to the ground. The plane, loaded with fuel, exploded on impact, killing all 277 people aboard instantly. Ultimately, the American Airlines maintenance crew was found to be at fault. They had failed to follow proper procedures when removing the engine and pylon during repairs and maintenance prior to this flight.

The stranger who had promised to meet them with his car never appeared. So Cheri and her friend caught a flight the next day, flew to L.A. and were greeted by her stepmother, Penny, and her dad. Penny was furious because they had seen the crash on the news before Cheri got around to calling them to say they had decided not to take that flight.

"Mom [Cheri always called Penny "Mom"] was so upset she slapped me," Cheri told me.

It occurred to me that my mother, faced with the same circumstances, would have hugged me tight, cried, and told me she loved me.

During the many hours Cheri and I talked about her life, I never lost the capacity to be gobsmacked by such anecdotes. I would be pulled up short by these matter-of-fact stories in which anger and affection were interchangeable. Like so many slaps in the face.

Chapter 7

Cunning, Baffling and Powerful

Before we go further with Cheri's story, which is about to plunge into some pretty dark places, including murder, it seems a good time to pause and consider what must, by now, be obvious.

Alcohol and drug abuse has played a big part in her life, starting at a young age and continuing through numerous "bottoms," the recovery world's term for that point in life when the alcoholic/addict experiences complete despair and utter demoralization, when it becomes painfully clear that sobriety is the only choice left, barring a downward spiral toward, eventually, death - by alcohol poisoning, a fall down the stairs, a car accident, cirrhosis, or suicide. Endless options.

It is a fatal disease.

In too many cases, suicide seems preferable to living a life without the one thing that has – for so long – made life bearable. But others do choose to live, to surrender to the fact that they are powerless over alcohol or drugs, that their lives "have become unmanageable," the language in the very first step of the 12 step programs that have saved millions of lives.

My life is one of those. I have accumulated, one day at a time, more than 30 years of sobriety. Cheri has managed to put together, collectively, almost two decades of sobriety, despite a few slips along the way. Although we did not know this about one another when we first started our collaboration, and although Cheri has had her struggles facing her past again during the writing of this book, our friendship has only deepened because of it. In fact, I am not at all sure I could have written this story without that common bond of rigorous honesty.

Here's why: people who have never experienced what it's like to be in thrall to alcohol and drugs, which is – in the language of recovery – "cunning, baffling and powerful," may *profess* to be sympathetic, may give lip service to the modern understanding of alcoholism as a disease or disorder, passed on from one generation to another. But sympathy is not empathy, and repeated failures on the part of the addict to "reform" are extremely frustrating to those around them.

"Why can't you just *stop*?" they ask, especially after witnessing numerous run-ins with the law, losing spouses and children, and -in Cheri's case – even her freedom. "What is it going to *take*?" people may wonder.

That depends, of course, on the person. I hit bottom, as they say, when I was a single mother in my 40's, embarking on a new and challenging career, overwhelmed by anxiety and stress. I could not stop "self-medicating" every day with alcohol and I had enough knowledge about the disease of alcoholism and its frequent occurrence in my family history to literally call for help. I had tried and tried to stop, but could not do it on my own. Demoralized and desperate, I dialed a number in the phone book and was directed to a meeting near my home, where approximately 300 sober (and those hoping to be sober) alcoholics were gathered. "My God," I thought, "the whole town is in recovery!" From the moment I raised my hand that night and identified as an alcoholic for the first time, I have not had another drink. Something about the simple act of surrendering and asking for help flipped a switch in my brain. It took me out of my stubborn (and always futile) hope that I could control this thing on my own, that it was just a matter of will power, which is what so many people still believe.

I have been around alcoholism and addiction long enough to know that not everyone is lucky enough to realize there is power in surrender, that it takes great courage to ask for help, and to realize it before they lose their job, their family, their freedom and, in some cases, their lives. Cheri's journey to a place where she could "surrender" was long, tortuous and extremely painful. After all, she had been taught to live by "the code" drilled into her by her father, a code that would not abide any hint of surrender or asking for help. This code came from the mind of the man she idolized, the same man who physically and emotionally abused her from an early age, a man who was, in Cheri's words, "a mean, mean drunk."

So it was important to me to pause long enough in the telling of her story to underscore how difficult it was for her to reach the awareness and humility needed in order for her to surrender and ask for help. Important because the next few years, starting with her second marriage and countless second chances marred by even more disastrous choices, are bound to elicit a few thoughts of "what is it going to *take*?" from those now following this story. And in Cheri's case, the answer will be "a lot more than most."

Addiction may help *explain* terrible behavior and horrific choices, but it does not *excuse* them. And Cheri would be the first to say so. Hers is a story of recovery because it is founded on a true and honest reckoning of what we call "the wreckage of our past." I am not at all sure, given the same circumstances in life, that I could have climbed over that same wreckage to find a new life. In the words of her ex-husband, Jerry Mathews, "The woman is a miracle. I don't know how many guardian angels are watching over her, but it's amazing."

Chapter 8

Looking for Love in All the Wrong, and Same, Places

"How many lifetimes has she lived? Unbelievable. She self-sabotaged because of her childhood messages, telling her she was worthless. How many 'fathers' has she had in her life who reinforced that message?"

—Cerise Laberge, former inmate with Cheri at Valley State Prison

"Can This Marriage Be Saved?" was the most widely read column in magazine history, featuring a different couple and their problems each month in *The Ladies Home Journal*, starting in 1954. I thought of that column when I talked to Cheri and Jerry Mathews – in separate conversations - about their tumultuous 5 years together, before their divorce in 1987. Their union probably never had a chance, even if they had had the means or inclination to try marriage counseling. In hindsight, of course, their inevitable collision course is plain to see. But it's safe to say their marriage could probably never have been "saved," as the pop psychology of a magazine column would put it, given their emotional baggage and their alcohol and drug addictions.

Nevertheless, both of them describe their initial meeting as "love at first sight." They met at a bar called the Rock Quarry in Junction City, Kansas, not far from the Army base where Cheri was based. Jerry told me, "I'll never forget it. When I saw her, my eyes lit up. We both lit up." Cheri had a similar physical reaction: "He was gorgeous, really built, had a great smile."

Before long, they were living together at his house in Junction City. Jerry, a civilian, worked for the railroad but their world revolved around a bar owned by Jerry's friends. "We partied constantly," says Cheri, "and we all got along real well."

Until they didn't.

Jerry's childhood made Cheri's look like something out of *The Brady Bunch*. When he was seven, his mother died and he and his three older siblings were left with his stepfather, a cop who physically abused them. They ran away and lived on the streets for the better part of two years. Jerry was eventually adopted at the age of 8, through the help of a local church. His luck seemed to turn at that point, when a kind couple in Ft. Riley, Kansas, Gerald and Carol Mathews, brought him home to live with them.

Cheri: Jerry's adoptive parents were great people. *Real* Christians. Hearts of gold. I loved them. I wish they had been my parents.

But the psychological damage of Jerry's early years would linger, and ultimately collide with Cheri's damaged psyche.

Cheri: We were drug addicts, alcoholics. Jerry had terrible abandonment issues from those early years, living on the streets, before he was adopted. And I was really co-dependent. "I can fix him, it's all my fault," that kind of thinking. And a lot of it *was* my fault. I had no idea how to love somebody. I made every man I was with insecure and jealous. Emotionally, I was not there. The first time he hit me, he backhanded me in front of his brothers. I got in my car and drove back to L.A. and got a job. But I missed him.

Jerry: I got a job working oil rigs in Kansas. I was devastated and missed her.

And so the pattern of breaking up, reconciling, drinking and drugging continued. They still weren't married. For a while, they lived in Northridge, California, where Jerry got a job as a roofer and Cheri worked for Sparkletts Bottled Water Company.

Cheri: I was the only woman working there. It was hard physical work, door to door sales and delivery. Jerry got his leg caught in a roofing conveyer and had to get skin grafts. One day, when Jerry had to go to the doctor, I went to play pool at a nearby bar with some people I worked with. Jerry walked in, grabbed me by the hair and dragged me outside. I fled to my parents' house, but he followed me. Told my dad I was a slut. I slapped Jerry, and he picked me up and threw me across the table. My dad was furious and went to get his knife. Jerry got on his knees, crying, "Just kill me. I can't live without her." Jerry packed his bag and I took him to the freeway. He was gone for a while on his own adventure, but sometime later he ended up at my Mom's place in Fallon.

I always thought something was wrong with *me*. I always felt defective. I had no idea what love looked like. I was capable of so much more, I think.

Jerry: I was always in love with her, but I couldn't take L.A. I got along real well with Cheri's mom, Carole. I always thought the dad and stepmom were sort of shady. Cheri's mom kept telling us to come to Fallon, Nevada, where she was living. So that's where we went.

Cheri: I got pregnant with Michelle, so we decided to get married. This was in Fallon in 1982. That's when the plane crash happened.

Judy: Another plane crash?

Cheri: This was a Harrier jet. It crashed in our yard. I wrote about it for one of my English classes when I went to prison.

Cheri wrote a lot of excellent essays for her classes in prison. And I say that as a former English teacher who has read a lot of student essays. One of her last instructors, when she was moved to the Women's Prison in Chino, was Leslie Van Houten, of Manson Family fame. But that's really just a footnote to the fact that Cheri could produce such good work, recalling the smallest details from her experiences. Almost all her essays, which she saved, earned her straight A's, including this one, which she titled "Snowball's Chance in Hell." She begins by describing how she and Jerry tried to put together a life in Fallon, Nevada. Cheri was pregnant with Michelle. She had stopped drinking and using because of the pregnancy. She describes their exodus from Los Angeles as "young refugees in search of asylum."

Asylum was granted in the form of a job managing a small cattle ranch on the outskirts of Fallon, Nevada. The one thorn in my side was two miles east of us, the Fallon Naval Air Station. Navy fighter pilots returning from their live-fire maneuvers used the ranch as a homing beacon to guide them back to the base's runways. My husband Jerry was enamored with the daily, impromptu air shows of screaming jets and bombers. Our pit bull, Snowball, not so much! I agreed with the dog, but after eight months I had come to accept them as part of the package. The noise was a small price to pay for a healthy environment to raise our first child, one month away from making her debut. In July of '83, a British-designed Harrier jet annihilated a good portion of the ranch.

What I heard, saw and did that day was based upon my belief that the ranch was being bombed, creating for me a terrifying reality that was no less real just because it wasn't true.

The morning dawned bright and uneventful. I watched Jerry leave for town through the window and laughed as Snowball, dejected at being left behind, found solace by rolling in the manure pile by the barn. "You're not coming in here," I thought, leaving the window to resume my letter writing. A quickly building rumble heralded the approaching squadron. As soon as they passed over, I heard a distinct whistling sound

I instantly identified (by years of watching war movies) as the sound of a dropping bomb. "That is too close if I can hear it," I thought. I headed back to the window.

.....

I looked out and the world exploded...and in a moment that felt like a lifetime, all thought, fear, and reaction ceased. Shock...turned me into a detached observer of some surreal dreamscape. Slow and utterly relentless, the massive rolling flame blotted out the sun, sky and life as it devoured everything in its path. Flaming projectiles of shrapnel shot out from the infernal nucleus...extending the devastation in all directions. The magnitude of what was happening suddenly registered as I realized that hell was heading straight for me.

I grabbed the phone, hitting 911 as I dove under the kitchen table. "They're bombing our ranch! They've got the wrong coordinates, Jesus fucking Christ, call the Air Station and tell them they've got the wrong coordinates!" I threw down the phone and grabbed the cold metal legs of our flimsy dinette table. Terror engulfed me as I heard the jets returning. I knew they were coming back to finish the job. Attempting a makeshift barricade, I crammed my swollen belly against the wall under the bar, dragging the table onto my back, gripping the legs for dear life. This could not really be happening. But it was. Unimaginable hopelessness and grief as I said goodbye to my unborn child.

Then the squadron passed and nothing happened. I was too scared to move until I heard the sound of sirens. Terror turned to panic as I remembered Snowball and fear for my dog drove me out the door into the black smoke. Desperately screaming Snowball's name amid the fires, I saw the fire trucks and troops arrive from the base.

All the spent terror and now grief over my dog turned to a seething rage. I verbally assaulted the first officer I saw. "You sons of bitches killed my dog! How could you be so fucking stupid? Find my dog now!" The officer backed up in surprise as this barefoot, pregnant, and screaming banshee seemed to appear from the fires of hell.

"I'm sorry, Ma'am, but there ain't a snowball's chance in hell your dog made it through that alive."

Of all the cliches, he just had to pick that one. I was fixing to sock him in his face when a rancher who lived down the road hollered, "Hey, lady, is your dog white?"

We found poor Snowball not far down the road, shaking uncontrollably under an old abandoned house. I cradled her in my arms and bawled my eyes out in gratitude and sudden exhaustion.

When we returned, the officers in charge informed me it was a plane crash and not a bombing raid. The paradigm shift was instantaneous.

I felt like an idiot and a coward.

The pilot came to see me the next day. He had been forced to eject as the plane began coming apart in midair. Battered and bruised, he was nonetheless overjoyed that I was all right.

"I tried to point the nose toward the irrigation ditch to slow it down before I bailed. The explosion blotted out the house and I was sure I'd killed someone." He couldn't have been any older than me, and I could see by the tears in his eyes that his terror had been as real as mine. I hugged him fiercely, amazed that we had all survived. That day was a profound lesson for me. Truth is relative. Belief creates my reality.

Cheri's encounter with a Harrier jet exploding in flames near her front door was a shockingly close call, but not a statistical anomaly. According to a 2002 report in the *L.A. Times*, 45 Marine pilots were killed in *noncombat* accidents in Harriers between 1971 and 2002. Informally referred to as the Harrier Jump Jet, it was named after a bird of prey. Some pilots called it "the widow maker" because of its high accident rate.

Cheri's encounters with various predators seem never-ending: a gaggle of mean girls, a handful of sociopaths, emotionally abusive parents, physically abusive spouses, one angry bear and a flaming jet plane. The strains of "A Predator in a Pear Tree" play in my head. But surely the most insidious has been the predation of low self-esteem, deeply embedded in that lonely girl who used to "go away" in her fantasies, dreading the abuse waiting for her every night, the lonely girl whose first instinct upon learning that she had mistaken a jet crashing in her yard for an errant bombing run is to say, "I felt like an idiot and a coward."

Chapter 9

When the Bough Breaks

There is a brief snapshot of happiness, a short dalliance with serenity, when Cheri first experiences motherhood. In this hopeful glimpse of possibility over probability, Cheri is clean and sober, "super-happy," in her words, to have a baby. In the memory she describes to me, she is sitting in the living room of a house they had moved to in the town of Fallon, miles away from the ranch and the horror of Harrier jets. Jerry is not there. He is staying in Elko, Nevada, some four hours away, where he has found work. Cheri is alone with Michelle, sitting in a rocking chair at 2 a.m., breast feeding her newborn daughter, watching the Mesquite rodeo being televised on a local channel, thinking of her best memories of her mother, who often competed in rodeo barrel racing. "I slept alone in the bed with the baby," she told me, safe to dream her best dreams, safe from cravings, safe from abuse.

Fallon has been a home base for members of the Mathews family for years now. First populated by Forty-Niners during the Gold Rush, it was a convenient resting place after crossing the Carson River, north of town, on the way to the California hills. Fallon was a waystation for migrants dreaming of riches just over the horizon, but it would come to represent something else to the Mathews family - a sense of hopeful permanence, a safe, familiar place to return to when yet another venture (or marriage) would dissolve like so much desert dust. It remains a small town, about 3 and half square miles, population just under 10,000 people, mostly white. Years after Cheri sat nursing Michelle in a state of relative serenity, years when she was serving a life sentence for murder, Jerry Mathews would remarry and raise the kids in Fallon.

Because of its desert climate, Fallon is a place of extremes - blazing hot in the summers and bitterly cold nights in the winter. It can also experience a heavy fog in winter, known as pogonip. The word is derived from a Shoshone word for cloud, and "Beware the Pogonip" is a warning that regularly popped up in *The Old Farmer's Almanac*. In one of Jack London's works, *Smoke Bellew*, a pogonip surrounds the main characters, killing one of them.

The pogonip seems an apt metaphor — pathetic fallacy alert! - for the menacing cloud that followed Cheri, once she left that cozy chair in a cozy house, and followed her husband to Elko so they could be together.

Jerry: We wanted to be good parents, so she came to Elko. But we got back into cocaine and drinking and then gambling took over.

Cheri: Once I got to Elko, I switched Michelle over to formula. And I started drinking again. Got a job at the Red Lion Hotel and Casino as a cocktail waitress. And I started gambling.

In recovery circles, multiple addictions are not uncommon. Some people call it the whack-a-mole effect: stop drinking, start eating. Or drugging. Or gambling. Anything to provide that hit of dopamine to the brain. Cheri's new addiction, fueled by alcohol and drugs and funded by her lucrative waitressing tips, took her into uncharted territory of reckless behavior.

Jerry and Cheri Mathews with daughter Michelle

Cheri: Jerry was a great Dad and took care of Michelle when I was at work. But he was also really jealous of my job as a cocktail waitress, wearing a skimpy dress, working late at night. The gambling got worse and Jerry and I were physically fighting again. And drinking. And using cocaine. I didn't want to go home at night. I'd gamble away all my tip money. I was addicted to the poker machines. 25 cents a game, 5 dollar maximum. You can lose a lot of money that way. Fast.

Jerry: When she touches a casino, it's like a drink.

Cheri's best friend from high school, Christina Karlen, remembered an incident that foreshadowed this addiction. I had not mentioned the gambling issue when I spoke with her, but she offered up a troubling memory on her own. "She had a gambling problem,

I think. We went to the local county fair and she became obsessed at this one booth, she was obsessed with winning this stuffed animal. She spent all her money at that booth. I couldn't get her to leave. She became incredibly agitated, saying 'I have to win this!' and refusing to stop until she lost everything."

Refusing to stop until she lost everything would become a pattern for years to come.

Then, right in the middle of this unresolved mess in Cheri's life, her father's own downward spiral sucked Cheri back into the maelstrom of her unresolved feelings for the man who had abused her for so many years. Robert Shaw's alcoholism had finally reached such a nadir that his family decided to stage an intervention, with the goal of getting him into a rehab facility. Cheri, who was deeply immersed in her own addictions, nevertheless took part, albeit long distance.

Cheri: I wrote him a letter from Elko, telling him all the ways he had abused us through his drinking. We all took part in the intervention and it worked. He agreed to go to the Betty Ford Center. But he was given a physical exam there and was diagnosed with terminal pancreatic cancer. He was 42 years old. So they sent him home.

I felt so guilty for writing that letter.

The death of her father, not surprisingly, had an enormous impact on Cheri. She shared this part of her story over the phone, as I typed away on the computer with my iPhone on "speaker" mode. In fact, most of our conversations were conducted this way during the pandemic summer and fall of 2020. That might seem limiting, but those of us who have worked in the medium of radio know very well that the voice can have a powerful impact, with pauses and stillness speaking more loudly than words or pictures. As Cheri paused at this juncture in her story, I heard the stifled sobs and uneven breathing of someone trying hard not to cry. It was one of the very rare moments when I would hear (or see) Cheri cry, and she is someone who had a lot to cry about. Watching her father die from terminal cancer over a period of some months triggered a confusing mixture of anger and grief. In fact, they were indistinguishable. The anger stemmed, in part, from what she saw as a violation of his own "code," the one hammered into her brain at a young age.

Cheri: He had a terrible last six months. And I couldn't understand why he accepted the chemo and radiation. He always said he would never go out that way. I know he was emotionally challenged, had his own personality disorders. But I always thought of him as that rock-hard man I idolized. What my Dad told me was embedded in me. Why did he fight so hard to stay alive? It was hard to watch. He fell in the shower and broke bones. It was terrible.

Judy: Did you visit him often during those six months?

Cheri: I did go back to see him in California a few times, but he would never talk about what was happening. He did stop drinking, but there were no final thoughts, no final words. We walked on eggshells, like there was nothing wrong. Which is not surprising, since that was always the way we communicated. After these visits, I would go back to Elko, still using drugs and drinking myself, and angry because he was dying. I missed being there for his actual death. He was 42 years old, and I was just 23, and we had never talked about our feelings. Not once. So many unresolved issues.

Judy: Still unresolved for you?

Cheri: I just wish I could have talked to him about these things. I have tried to forgive my Dad. He loved my mother, was obsessed with her betrayal, and I looked just like her. I didn't know better. He didn't know better. Poor Penny, who gave her life for that family. He did his best and his best was so terrible. While he was dying, he refused to accept it, so I didn't accept it either. The finality of it was overwhelming.

Judy: Was there a funeral?

Cheri: Yes. I flew back from Elko. A lot of people showed up for it. He hated most of these people. I took two Quaaludes, stood up at the funeral, and told them to get the hell out of there, told them my dad had never liked them. It was an embarrassing moment for Penny and the family. I was unleashed, acting out my anger, my rage. Poor Penny. I apologized later. Penny sold the house and the gas station and bought a new Cadillac. Never shared any of the money with me or Susie or even Mandy. She didn't tell us she was doing that. At first, I didn't care. Never did, really. It just hurt to think she wouldn't tell me.

Her father's death was definitely a turning point for Cheri. And not in a good way.

Cheri: I just wanted my dad back. I was married with a baby. I wanted a life of my own, wanted him to see that, wanted to please him. I always wanted to please him. I loved my dad. After the Army, he finally treated me like an equal. He did cocaine with me, we drank together.

Again, that slap-in-the-face moment of compare and contrast. I miss and love my dad, too. We fished together.

Cheri: In Elko, the gambling got worse. And the drinking and the fighting. Michelle was just a baby. So we decided we had to move to get me away from casinos. We went back to Kansas.

Judy: That sounds like you were "taking a geographic," as the saying goes.

Cheri: Right. But as we know, wherever you go, there you are. As the saying goes.

Jerry and Cheri took 2-year-old Michelle back to Kansas, to live near his parents. Jerry went to work as a delivery truck driver for Coca-Cola, and Cheri was able to buy a house with a VA loan.

Cheri: I got pregnant, so I stopped drinking again. We didn't have much money, so Jerry told me we couldn't afford pre-natal care. Jerry was still drinking. And he was so jealous. One night I went out with the girls to a bar. Jerry drove up and threw a drink in my face in the parking lot. He was calling me a "fucking whore" when the cops drove up and he took off. I was sober and pregnant

and crying in the back of the cop car. I never cheated on him, never. I later found out that he had cheated on me. Twice.

At seven months pregnant, I had a bad fall while I was water skiing. I have always wondered if that affected the birth. Our son Jason was born breach. I broke blood vessels in my face and chest, I was pushing so hard. The cord was around his neck, he was deep blue, no crying. Folded in half like a jackknife. The doctor finally got him to cry. For a short while, it turned into a happy thing.

Judy: And?

Cheri: He was born without tear ducts. He had to have surgery as a newborn so he wouldn't go blind. They told us there was a 50-50 chance he could die during the surgery. It took six hours and the recovery was brutal. I had to push the tear ducts every day to get fluid out. And he would scream with pain. Michelle tried to pick him up and dropped him on the floor, which caused a big knot to bulge out of his neck. They said it was a muscle spasm from when he was folded up inside me. So he had to move his neck in physical therapy, which was very painful.

I loved the kids. So did Jerry. He had to babysit a lot because I had to take two jobs waitressing after he got laid off. He whined all the time, which brought me down. So we fought.

Michelle was three years old when Cheri and Jerry fought for the last time as a married couple. They had managed to keep the domestic violence piece of their marriage hidden from friends. Cheri says neither of them ever laid a hand on the kids, determined to avoid an encore of their own childhoods.

Cheri: Nobody we knew had any idea that he laid hands on me. Only Penny knew, and she hated him for it. His parents, who I loved, never saw it. I would cover up bruises on my arms and throat. The fight that ended it for us was after a kids party, where the moms played cards and drank. When I came home, my friend Sheila drove me and came into the house. Jerry just walked over and hit me, hard. I fell into our collection of beer steins and broke them. Sheila jumped on Jerry's back and tried to stop him.

Now somebody close to us knew and had seen it.

Sheila told my friends. That was the moment of truth. It was never going to stop. No matter how often we moved, HE was never going to stop.

Judy: And that was your moment of truth about the marriage?

Cheri: Yes. I blamed myself.

Judy: What?

Cheri: I was failing at my marriage. I should have changed my behavior. But I didn't want to divorce like my parents. I didn't want to lose my kids. But I knew I had to end the marriage, so I told him we were getting a divorce.

Judy: His reaction?

Cheri: He ran off with all the money from the bank account. Finally called me from another state, crying, scared to death, saying he wanted to kill himself. But he could be so manipulative. "I'll never do it again," was the refrain, followed by the honeymoon period. Then it would start all over.

Not this time. Jerry and Cheri both hired lawyers and got a divorce. She received 200 dollars a month in child support and custody of the kids. But Cheri had trouble keeping up the payments on the house, so in the end, she sold it and left for California with her stepmom, Penny, who had bought a home in Lake L.A., California, in the desert near Lancaster. Yet another chance to put her life together. Yet another chance to blow it.

Cheri: I fell in love again. With meth.

Chapter 10

"You Lose Your Soul"

Unlike Cheri, I have never tried methamphetamine. I was never tempted to, mostly because the descriptions of the drug's effects horrified me. Alcohol was my drug of choice, because I was looking to chill out and slow down, not speed up. And it worked just fine, until it didn't. But meth is another story, occupying a universe all its own, a universe where Cheri landed with a bang, long before she landed in prison. A simple google search about meth addiction yields a horrific list of symptoms and side effects. "The extreme psychological and physical toll that meth takes on the body makes it one of the most dangerous drugs on the market," reads one medical website, listing some of the symptoms as hyperactivity, twitching, paranoia, weight loss, skin sores, agitation, erratic sleeping patterns, rotting teeth and mood swings. Another telling symptom is "tweaking," a period of anxiety and insomnia that can last for days, usually at the end of a drug binge. "Tweakers" are desperate to score more of the drug, and can become prone to violent behavior and hallucinations.

What fun! But addicts who get hooked on meth are not likely to google the drug's deleterious effects. Or even want to. They take it because the hits of dopamine, euphoric and energizing, just keep on coming. It can be snorted, smoked or injected. Cheri started by snorting it.

Cheri: You could do one line and stay high for days. 100 dollars a gram. 250 dollars for an eight ball. It's *speed*. You're happy, productive, going a hundred miles an hour. Spotless home, great yard, great ideas! Lots of talking, going too fast, staying up for days.

That initial euphoric rush lasts longer than other drugs, a main part of the appeal. But it eventually fades, leading to intense drug cravings and depression. As the body crashes, deprived of the dopamine that meth was supplying, the brain is fixated on more, more, more. Addicts gradually give up those areas of life that were once important. Like relationships.

Cheri: I've gone for two weeks without sleep. I was tweaking in a thrift store for hours. Unable to stop, sweating, buying bags of stuff. Tweaking is the *behavior* on meth. This is when people start stealing. I couldn't let meth friends into my house. I would be missing stuff.

Now that she was divorced, with custody of the kids, living in Lake L.A., California with Penny, Cheri had another shot at building a life free of gambling, drug abuse and domestic abuse. But meth entered the picture, and she was off and running.

In the opposite direction.

Cheri: Meth takes over your life. You lose your soul. It was fast. I was so out of control that I called Jerry and asked him to come and get the kids. I moved from Penny's house to a friend's house in Lancaster. It was a blur of drinking and using and waking up in strange places, sometimes with no car or clothes. A lot of blackouts.

Still, some sort of survival instinct kicked in, yet again. Cheri gave up her fling with meth (at least temporarily) and moved back home to Fallon, Nevada, to live with her Mom, Carole, and Carole's fifth husband, Doug. She got a job as a waitress at Stockman's Steakhouse (and casino) but then proceeded to prove that old adage, "insanity is repeating the same behavior over and over and expecting different results." Although she and Jerry were already divorced, they decided to give it another try, moving into a trailer together with the kids. She had stopped using meth (at least for that period of time), but both she and Jerry were snorting coke and drinking. And the physical fighting started up again.

I don't remember how many instances there were but there were a lot. We even stopped using and drinking for a while but it didn't make any difference. Our last fight happened when I was getting ready for work. Jerry came in the bathroom and started by ripping my shirt off. It went on through the house to the bedroom. He had me on the bed and he wrapped the phone cord around my throat. He called 911 and threatened to kill me and himself. The police came to the trailer and took Jerry away. The D.A. charged him but I told the D.A. to please drop the charges. He said he would if I left Jerry. So the kids and I left and I got a low income apartment.

By this chapter in her narrative, I have stopped counting all the "second chances."

Judy: At some point, alcoholics and drug addicts hit a final "bottom." And they hit it, if they are lucky, while they still have a life. Long before we reached this point in your story, I began to wonder when that would ever happen for you. And to you.

Cheri: Judy, my bottoms have bottoms.

And so we plunge, once again, into the muck and mire of addiction. Cheri was working at Stockman's Steakhouse and Casino when she got drunk one night and gambled away all her money. Her rage at herself, fueled by alcohol, prompted her to punch in the glass door of the casino, punch in the windshield of her own car, and – on the way home to her mom's house — sideswipe a guardrail over the river.

Mom covered the bill for the glass window at the casino to keep me out of jail. Then she and Doug took me to Truckee Meadows Psychiatric Center.

At Truckee, Cheri had the rare luxury of taking a few weeks for a "time out," including frequent sessions with a psychiatrist, something she had never before experienced. He put her on Thorazine, often prescribed for bipolar disorder and schizophrenia, and Lithium, also used to treat bipolar disorder and suicidal depression.

The psychiatrist kept working with me on my father hang-ups. I had blocked out a lot of my childhood, and he told me I have issues with my sexuality. He said he knows there is something more, something I may have blocked out. One day, I was in the TV room alone and I was watching the John Bradshaw tapes about the dysfunctional family. All of a sudden, I'm a little girl again. Like 7 or 8 years old. And I'm lying sideways on a table with my knees up and I am being held down. My pants are off and Richard H. is sexually assaulting me. I can feel everything like it's happening to me right then and I really freak out. I'm so angry and I'm screaming. How could I have forgotten that happened? And I realized it happened more than once. It happened to Susie, too, and she was only 4.

Richard and his brothers lived down the street from Cheri when she was growing up in Van Nuys, California. Their mother was Penny's best friend, which is why Cheri and Susie were often in their house. She believes Penny must have found out about the frequent sexual abuse and put an end to it, but that she never told Bob Shaw, Cheri's father, because she knew he would have killed those boys. At least, that's what Cheri believes now. In her recounting of this repressed memory in her prison biography, she had a different explanation.

After the initial shock and anger that anyone could do that to a little girl had worn off, I felt a hopeful relief that my dad must have known and he couldn't handle what happened so he raised me to make sure that it would never happen again.

That's a pretty torqued rationale for the mental and physical abuse she suffered at the hands of her father, the idea that he had to harshly discipline her in order to protect her. And she eventually gave up on that theory, because it was much more plausible to believe that Penny had feared sharing this secret, knowing that Bob Shaw would have gone ballistic. A Hobson's Choice: either your step mother was protecting those boys, after they had repeatedly assaulted you sexually, or your father knew about it and decided to raise you with draconian cruelty, to protect you from men and sex. Or, more to the point, to keep you "from being a whore like your mother." Serious psychological issues, either way. John Bradshaw's self-help tape, *Family Secrets: The Path from Shame to Healing,* may have reignited a repressed memory, but Cheri would never have the luxury of working out those knotty questions under the care of a mental health professional. And self-help was not on the menu. She was discharged from Truckee Psychiatric Hospital with a prescription for Thorazine and Lithium. She had been court-ordered to attend meetings of Alcoholics Anonymous.

So now I'm in that low income apartment with the kids again and I'm working at the Yellow Unicorn restaurant as a waitress. I am taking evening college classes in Philosophy and U.S. Government at the local community college. I am not taking drugs but I am drinking again, so I'm a closet drinker going to AA meetings. Obviously, the meetings are having no impact because I am drinking a 6-pack of beer before I go to class. That makes it much easier to communicate with the teachers. I love the arguments in class and I get good grades.

I also get a DUI one night. And after losing my license, I get another summons for driving on a suspended license. I ignore them. I never show up to take care of those tickets, so now there is a warrant out for me. I ignore that, as well.

That would prove to be a serious oversight.

One night, when she was gambling in a local casino in Fallon, Cheri's mom, Carole, came looking for her, angry that Cheri was once again gambling away all her money, money they had planned to spend on a vacation together.

My mom come into the casino and goes all drama on me. We are certified scuba divers and we are saving up for a trip to Cancun for a month of diving. My half-brother Ronnie was planning to go, too. I'm pissed at her because I'm drunk and I'm winning. I tell her it's a little late to play Mommy now. I see the hurt on her face, and she leaves. The next morning, after a long night of drinking, I went to her restaurant (the Yellow Unicorn) and went off on my Mom, yelling and carrying on. I quit my waitressing job. And left town.

Susie and I got a house in Reno together, with my kids. I got a job at the Clarion Hotel and Casino as a cocktail waitress.

Another "geographic," another round of repeating the same behavior and expecting different results. The results, at this point, are tragically predictable. Cheri's gambling addiction was fueled by good tips at her new job at a casino, one-stop shopping, and she once again gambled away all of her money, returning home in the mornings just in time to get the kids up.

This whirlwind of insanity finally climaxed in a terrible fight with her sister, Susie, a person with so many of her own problems that a collision was just a matter of time. And this time, the eruption of anger and self-loathing triggered a suicide attempt by a now-seriously depressed Cheri.

I swallowed all my Thorazine and Lithium and ran out the door. Ronnie [their half-brother had moved in with them] *called the cops and they found me on the street, losing consciousness, when the ambulance got there and they pumped my stomach. I woke up in the hospital. My stepdad, Ron, was sitting next to the bed. Then Susie walked into the room.*

She said one thing. "The rent is due. I need your paycheck."

Judy: That's all? You've just attempted suicide and those are the first words you hear when you wake up?

Cheri: She could be a hateful little shit.

Judy: What happened to the kids?

Cheri: Jerry came to get them, and moved them to Kansas. I signed over primary custody to him. Michelle was 7, Jason 5.

(Long pause)

Cheri: I am now continuing my slide to a seemingly bottomless bottom.

The outstanding warrant for driving on a suspended license is still out there, and so is the meth, both patiently waiting to pounce, like so many pogonips swirling in the desert.

Chapter 11

"....Just Like Your Mother"

I quit my job [in Reno] because it was worthless for me to work in a casino. I packed a suitcase and left everything else behind and started hitchhiking. I didn't know what I was doing and I didn't care. A guy and a girl picked me up and gave me a ride. The girl – I remember her name was Cherry – asked me if I'd ever been a prostitute. I said no and she offered to get me a job at a brothel, Kitty's Brothel outside Carson City, where she worked.

Judy: Seriously? A girl named *Cherry* offered you a job in a brothel?

Cheri: Yes. Really. And I was so hopeless, I thought "why not?" I had just gotten out of the hospital from my suicide attempt, I had lost my kids, I had nothing left. So she took me to work with her.

Judy: And this is legal, right, because it's Nevada?

Cheri: Yes. It was a bunch of trailers put together behind a locked fence. We were beeped in, and I entered this big lobby with red velvet sofas, with nude pictures on the wall, and met Kitty, the madam. Cherry was one of their top earners, cute and young. Prostitution is big business in Nevada.

Judy: Red velvet sofas, nudes on the wall, a madam named Miss Kitty. Right out of a B-movie. Or X-rated movie.

Cheri: Yeah. (laughing) Bordello Chic.

Judy: Was there an "interview?"

Cheri: Basically, I just had to fill out a 1099 tax form, get a physician's card and a police card, to be on file in the house. They paid for all that. At this point, I was not a felon, so I had a clean record. Kitty told me how things worked, that I was a "subcontractor." She told me police would come by periodically to check on my papers. We would get examined by a doctor once a week. It's big business in Nevada. There were three other whore houses in the same neighborhood. This was in Dayton, just outside Carson City.

Judy: How were you feeling about all this?

Cheri: When I first walked in, I thought, "They won't want me. I have no boobs, I'm not very attractive." I was pretty insecure. They showed me to my room. I remember sitting on the edge of my bed, alone, and thinking "Well, here I am, Dad." I had such a feeling of fate, of living out my Dad's predictions for me, such despondency and hopelessness. For my whole life.

Judy: So how did you manage to do this work with no experience, especially when you were feeling so depressed?

Cheri: Kitty assured me that, as a "subcontractor," I could refuse to do things I did not want to do, as long as I did it tactfully. For example, you could say "well, that would be 500 dollars extra" and they would drop whatever weird request they had in mind.

Judy: Was there was a set rate?

Cheri: Here's how it worked. When a customer would walk in, a buzzer would go off, and all the girls who did not have a "party" booked would go to the lobby and line up together. The guy could choose a girl or stay in the lobby and party with all the girls. The fee started at 100 dollars an hour. Some girls charged 200. A hand job or blow job was just 50 dollars. For S and M – 400 an hour.

On the first night there, they supplied me with a sexy tight dress. But I was barefoot, because they didn't have size 10 heels to fit me. The first fucking customer picked me. Over all those other pretty girls!

Judy: You sound as though you were flattered.

Cheri: I was, in a way, until I found out later that the customers had heard I was the new girl. New girls are naïve, they work hard for the money. I screwed ten guys that night. Could hardly walk the next day. The girls told me "Cheri, you cannot keep doing this" and proceeded to tell me the tricks for wasting time during that hour. How to delay the sex.

Judy: Such as?

Cheri: A lot of talk. After the guy picks you, you have to make an agreement on the money you are going to charge. You take them to your room, where they have to pull down their pants so you can make sure they have no disease or sores. You decide the fee and then walk back to the office, hand over the money (the house took 50%) and you pick up the rubbers you need. Then you go back to the room, wash their genitals with bacterial soap and try to talk them into going into the jacuzzi first. It eats up time, and also you know they are really clean. Once their hour is up, a maid knocks on the door. The maids were really like enforcers, kicking people out when the time was up or insisting on more money being charged if the client wanted to stay and finish. They were strong women, strong enough to handle trouble from clients.

Judy: It sounds dangerous. On a lot of levels.

Cheri: Only once. A guy actually tried to rape me. My mistake. He wanted to tie me up and I let him. Then he wanted anal sex, which I refused. He didn't listen. I screamed for help and the "maids" and some of the other girls who heard me screaming came running in to take care of him.

Judy: How did they do that?

Cheri: They attacked him with their high heels. Those spike heels were great as weapons. You could do a lot of damage. He was chased out of the place by a bunch of women slashing at him with high heels.

Judy: But you stayed, even after this scary attempted rape.

Cheri: My self-esteem got better while I was there. Customers would pay a lot to see me, buy me gifts. One even wanted to marry me and stay with him. One guy paid to give me oral sex, wanted nothing in return. One truck driver just liked to spend the night, to talk and cuddle. I could feel his need for connection, talking about our dreams, our children. My heart softened and I became friends with these people. And the other girls were so supportive.

Judy: You mentioned that some of the women were married? How did that work?

Cheri: Their husbands were their pimps. Those girls tended to be seasonal workers, working through the ski season, then taking off months at a time. We got a lot of young skiers as clients. You know, "We're in Nevada, might as well go to a whore house after we hit the slopes!" If I could open a whore house in Telluride, I'd make a bundle!

Cheri burst into laughter at this idea, imagining that unlikely scenario. Of course, not only would that be illegal in Colorado, but also a major parole violation. But I had to admit, the idea of an upscale whorehouse in the midst of all those multi-million dollar homes sounded like a pretty good pitch for a Netflix series. Clearly, the pandemic was wearing on me.

Judy: Aside from skiers, who else made up your clientele?

Cheri: All types. I had a cop once. Truck drivers, construction workers, businessmen. Mostly young, not a lot of old fogey pervs, like you would imagine. Women were not allowed in. Too many jealous wives out there. Inside, we had a good life. We used aliases instead of our real names. Mine was Yvonne.

It was like a sisterhood, with all the girls looking out for one another.

Judy: Sounds like a sorority, of sorts.

Cheri: Yeah. It was a whole different paradigm for me. The outside world did not exist. You could buy clothes from the house. You never had to leave. The food was great. Every morning you had a formal breakfast with the madam, with china and linens. The maids served us. It was like one big family, in a nice house. Avon came calling on a regular basis. We had protection and we made good money. Only one girl specialized in S and M. I remember one day, when some of us were sitting in the bar having drinks, we watched her drag a guy out into the snow in his underwear and just leave him there, tied up like a calf and gagged. She dragged him out by his dog collar, then came in and had drinks with us, while we all watched him shivering in the snow. At the end of the hour, she brought him back in. 400 dollars for that! But he left happy. He was suffering and that's what turned him on.

Judy: Were you ever tempted to do anything like that?

Cheri: I did drip hot wax on a guy once. He loved it. I also tied up his balls with his shoe laces, so tight that he was in real pain. But it was hard for me to do those things. I really don't like to hurt people.

Judy: How long were you there?

Cheri: Four months. During that time, I started selling cocaine, provided by a local dealer. Most of my customers were the girls in the house. My sister Susie and I had reconciled and she was allowed to visit, and she was also a cocaine customer.

Judy: So you were making good money, between the drugs and the prostitution?

Cheri: I was still gambling. Customers could take you out on a date for a thousand dollar fee. But we would go gambling and I would lose money. Then Kitty warned me about selling drugs out of her house, which was a big no-no. So I knew it was time to go.

Chapter 12

We're Not in Kansas Any More

After four months of working at Kitty's, Cheri had saved enough money to fly to Kansas, where Jerry had moved with the kids. They were living in Junction City, near his parents. Cheri moved in with a pal from her Army days, "Kit" Carson, in Independence, Missouri, just across the state line. Her real name is Crystal, but Cheri had always known her as "Kit."

Kit: We'd always stayed in touch, so when she was through working in the whore house in Nevada, I had her come stay with me. "Come back," I told her, "I don't have much, but you can have what I've got."

Judy: That's a generous offer.

Kit: Back in the Army, she basically took care of me. I was young and dumb as a pile of rocks, living in a dump of a trailer. Cheri invited me to live with her. We hung out with the gang at the Rock Quarry Bar, then we moved in with Jerry. She was the house mom. We all partied and drank and did drugs, but she was the one who kept it all together.

Judy: Interesting perspective, because she came from a pretty abusive home, and she had a rough go, initially, in the Army.

Kit: By the time I met her, she was driving for the colonel and was doing fine. She only told me the good parts of her childhood,

the golden parts, like working on cars with her dad. We were both readers, really into books.

Judy: It had been about 8 or 9 years since you'd shared a house. How did the reunion go?

Kit: She wasn't the same old Cheri. Her drinking was heavier. She got a job as a waitress, but didn't make enough money so started hooking again, as an "escort." We had conversations about hooking, about quitting, but Cheri is strong-willed. She would down a six-pack watching TV, then pass out with a cigarette in her hand. Dangerous stuff. She ran with a wilder crowd than me.

Judy: Cheri says she tried to see her kids on the weekends, even it meant taking a bus to get to them.

Kit: She loved those kids. That's why she left them with Jerry. She knew she could not take care of them.

Judy: So what happened to the shared living arrangement?

Kit: I had to tell her she couldn't stay there anymore. It was a safety issue. I had cats and she was careless about the way she left cocaine around the place. She would cut lines of coke on my glass picture frames and just leave them there.

Judy: What did you say to her?

Kit: "This is not working for me. I don't feel safe with you here."

Judy: That must have been hard, given how you two started out years before that.

Kit: She moved out and lived in a rathole on Highway 40, a motel that had been turned into "apartments." I went to see her there and it was horrible. Moldy and dirty and nasty. So I gave her money for a bus ticket back to Nevada.

Judy: You rescued her, basically?

Kit: It's not like I was "rescuing" Cheri. I was doing what she had done for me when I was a kid in the Army. I would have gotten into way more trouble without her. She was always taking care of me, the big sister. Always there. She could cook, clean, knew how to take care of things. How to DO things. But you didn't fuck with her.

Judy: What do you mean?

Kit: I would see her ball up, get in someone's face, and they would back down. I remember a guy who we overheard in a bar talking about "doing crystal." And she balled up and was getting ready to jack him. She swung at him and I grabbed her arm. "Cheri," I said, "He's talking about doing meth, not me." We had a good laugh over that.

Judy: Could you have predicted that she would end up in prison for murder?

Kit: No way, shape or form. I could never have foreseen what would happen to her.

Judy: When did you last see her?

Kit: The last time I saw her she was in prison in California. I had relatives in Chowchilla, so I went to see her twice. I still remember her as the nurturer and protector. (long pause) I'm happy she's happy. I'm happy she survived.

But happiness, at *that* juncture, was still a long way off.

Cheri: Around that time in 1989, after my stay in Kansas, my stepmom Penny died in a car accident, leaving 14- year-old Mandy alone. Penny owned a place in Pinion Hills, California, a nice home. Penny's stepparents made a decision to put the house up for sale, even though it did not belong to them. Mandy called me from Truckee Meadows Psych ward! She told me they had committed her and were trying to sell her mom's house. I called and told them Mandy and I were keeping the house and that I was coming to California. So I flew back, talked to the lawyers to find out how to keep the house, since I shared the estate with Mandy. Penny had adopted me (but not Susie), so I was the legal heir along with my little sister.

That's what got me back to the fucking desert again. And meth.

Chapter 13

"Livin' La Vida Loca"

Apologies for planting that earworm. But at this juncture in Cheri's story, the frantically-paced hit that *Rolling Stone* once placed on their list of the "20 Most Annoying Songs" of the year makes for the perfect theme. Her frantic *vida* was definitely *loca*, but it nevertheless had a veneer of stability, much like a Western movie set has a veneer of stability, a solid front masking shaky supports. The pace was speedy, in every sense of the word.

Initially, Cheri had yet another chance to get it together. It was 1990, she was only 30 years old and she had just inherited a nice chunk of cash from Penny's estate. She and her young sister Mandy divided up the insurance payout and Cheri moved into the house, a four-bedroom, spacious place in Pinion Hills, in the desert near Lancaster. Mandy told me she just couldn't stay in that house without her mom there.

Mandy: For about a year and a half, I stayed with friends of my Mom. I love Cheri, she is my favorite sister. She was so amazing, always held her own. She had been through a lot, but she was strong.

Judy: And your sister Susie?

Mandy: Susie introduced me to drugs. When I was about 15, I had to go to rehab. I didn't realize how bad Susie was at first. My

mom tried so hard with Susie when she was younger, but it was already too late. Mom did not include her in the payouts from the insurance.

With Mandy living safely with friends, Cheri set about doing what came naturally - cleaning and keeping house. Manically and maniacally, courtesy of meth. And now that she owned a four-bedroom home in Pinion Hills, she thought she had it made. She paid her ex-husband Jerry the delinquent amount she owed in child support, $1500, and he agreed to let the kids come live with her in California.

I was in heaven! I never went back to work. I started selling drugs and met people who were doing the same thing. I was a single woman living in a remote area and selling meth. The meth always gave me courage and spontaneity that I would never had had sober.

Cheri wrote about this critical turning point in her life for an English class in prison. The essay was entitled "Buried Secrets."

An inheritance in 1990 left me with a home in the high desert and enough money to get a drug addict into trouble. They say that water seeks its own level, and it was not long before I fell in with the local "tweakers." I took what was left of my money, bought a shitload of methamphetamine, and opened for business. I now had the American Dream: big home, nice car, cute boyfriend and two great kids.

So, the boyfriend. Among the friends she invited to stay in the house, a handsome young man named Joey soon became a fixture. And her lover.

Cheri: He was so good-looking it was scary. Like a Greek god. Golden curly hair, blue, blue eyes. Sicilian/Scandinavian parents. He started coming over a lot. He was a plumber, 7 years younger than me. At first, the relationship was wonderful. But by the time Joey showed up, I was already dealing meth. And we started doing meth together on a regular basis. He started missing work and lost his job. So he started dealing meth with me.

Judy: And the kids?

Cheri: Michelle was 7 and Jason was 5. I got them into school. I loved having my kids. They had been living in a trailer with Jerry, but now they were living in a four bedroom house. I bought them lots of stuff. My house was nice and I kept it that way.

It was a time of magical thinking, a time she also described in her prison biography.

I was able to be home with the kids and had their friends over a lot. I would pick them all up from school and we would go 4-wheeling and get ice cream. We'd go to Magic Mountain on the weekends and I could afford to take them and all their friends. I wasn't used to having extra money and I wasn't wise with it at all. I was able to help out people when they needed it and that was a good feeling. The kids pretty much had everything they needed materially. But they still didn't have a sober, "present" mother. I was always cleaning or busy and seldom just sat with them.

Judy: So you were dealing and using this whole time?

Cheri: I never stopped to STOP. And THINK. Or GET HELP. It was one long, out-of-control ride. I loved the kids but I didn't know how to be a mother. I chose drugs over my kids time and time again. And I was tweaking, so I was often up all night. And paranoid from meth. Up on the roof with binoculars, looking for attackers. I dug a foxhole in our yard, waiting for people who had threatened Joey. We were both dealing. The cooking came later.

Among Cheri's tweaker friends in Pinion Hills was a guy named Ray Harrison. Today, he says, he is clean and sober, helping others who are trying to recover, and working for the Carpenter's Union. But back then, he was a wild young man, a friend of Joey's. And wishing Cheri had a crush on him instead.

Ray: I was in love with Cheri. But I could see why a girl would be attracted to Joey. He was good-looking, he learned how to make the meth. He was the man. But he was weak. He was tough only when he had a gun or when he was with tough people. I wanted to scream at Cheri, "Hey! What about this standup, badass guy in front of you!?"

Judy: And she never noticed?

Ray: She kissed me once, on her birthday. I was like a teenager, didn't know what to say. I had such a crush on her.

Judy: What was special about her?

Ray: She was so good-looking, and she was also that girl guys want. She could shoot a pistol, rebuild a motor, frame a new roof on her shed with a nail gun. Oh my God, I loved her! She had all these worldly skills, AND she was beautiful.

When I related Ray's comments to Cheri, she dismissed the idea that he was romantically infatuated with her. She chalked it up to the day he dropped by and saw her fixing her roof with a nail gun, wearing only a bikini and a tool belt.

Meanwhile, their days of youthful infatuation and bravado were about to end.

Ray: We were all young, thought we were tough. And then Frank came along. I'm not usually fearful, but Frank was a scary dude. He had a lifetime of hurting people. He just blew in one day. He was dark and dangerous. A total psychopath who fed off people's suffering.

(Long pause)

Cheri had no choice, you know? I would have done the same thing.

Chapter 14

The Killing Of Frank Belize

There is a saying in Alcoholics Anonymous: " you are only as sick as your secrets." I had secrets in my past that I buried a long time ago, but the grave was shallow and the damn things kept digging their way out. Childhood molestation and abuse morphed into abusive relationships, prostitution, and a variety of vices in my later years. Rather than face my demons, I covered them with drugs and alcohol. The hole I was digging with my consistent denial of reality was shaping itself into another grave, this time a real one. In 1993, I killed a man in self-defense.

—From Cheri's prison essay, "Buried Secrets"

In 1993, Cheri was living in that lovely house in Pinion Hills with her two children, her boyfriend Joey, a friend of Joey's named Tony, and a couple, Bo and Heather. One day, Cheri and Joey met a guy hanging out at the local gas station by the name of Frank Belize. He said he had just been released from prison in Chino and needed a place to stay for a while. Cheri, who prided herself on helping the less fortunate, invited him to stay at her house.

What could go wrong?

Everything, as it turned out.

We were all young and dumb and trying to be tough and cool. Frank, on the other hand, was a straight up, bona fide bad guy. It was like dropping a shark into a bowl of minnows.

According to Cheri's description of Frank Belize in her prison writings, he *wore a long coat and was pierced and tattooed everywhere and Joey followed him around like a puppy. I was ashamed of Joey because he was acting like Frank's punk.*

Frank was a player and we were his fiddle. What started out as subtle, subversive mind games soon became a blatant and hostile takeover of our lives. He went to work turning us against one another. He told Heather that he thought Bo and I had something going. He told Bo that Joey and Heather had something going. Things were missing from my house and Frank made a huge scene accusing Tony of stealing stuff. People were suspicious of one another and the energy was bad. We found out later he was committing burglaries and storing stuff in a shed.

Judy: And the kids were there all that time?

Cheri: Yes. It was creepy, because Frank was real good with my kids. I knew I had to get him out, but I had to be careful. He was a sociopath. He had a wife and child hiding from him in Kansas City. He said he would kill her when he found them, and I believed him. I remember standing in the kitchen listening to him talk, and I thought of Michael Keaton in the movie, "Pacific Heights." It was that kind of evil manipulation.

["Pacific Heights" was a 1990 psychological thriller starring Keaton as a sociopathic tenant who works to drive out his landlords, a married couple, by setting them against one another.]

Judy: So what tipped the scales for you?

Cheri: I made the mistake of talking about how angry I was with this couple I knew, Mac and Terri, who owed me $500. I had given them the money to pick up an ounce of meth for me. They got ripped

off, and my $500 was gone. I was really mad, but I shouldn't have run my mouth off in front of Frank.

Judy: What happened?

Cheri: Frank and Joey went over to their house, to get my money back. Frank cracked open Terri's head with the butt of a gun and shot off the side of Mac's face and his ear. He tied them up and was going to kill them, but Joey convinced him not to. This was the moment when Joey became truly afraid of Frank.

I had already told Frank he would have to leave, but now Frank thinks I "owe him." They [Joey and Frank] came back that night with jewelry and loot they had taken from Mac and Terri's. Frank dumped it on the floor. He was covered in blood, cranked up, talking about it, excited. He loved to hurt people.

Judy: Did the couple report the assault?

Cheri: Yes. The police came to my house and demanded to know where Frank and Joey were. They were hiding inside, but I wouldn't let them in without a warrant.

I wanted to protect Joey, but also I could never snitch on anyone, not even Frank.

Judy: The "code" again?

Cheri: Of course the code! Ever since my mom stopped talking to me, cutting me off when I was 12 for snitching on her, I vowed to live by my father's code and never do such a thing again. I become my dad when I'm on meth, and every "teaching" is amplified on meth.

The cop said, "You are going to regret this." I remember that. I remember those words.

After the police left, I took Joey and Frank to a motel in Victorville and rented them a room. Joey decided to turn himself in and went to the Victorville jail. Later, I was leaving my house and someone took a shot at me. Mac had tried to have someone kill me. I had two kids in the house and I'd had enough. So I went to Mac and Terri's house by myself, carrying a gun. They had people guarding the outside of their house and they walked me in. I saw Mac and I wanted to cry. His head

was one big bandage. I told them I had nothing to do with what Frank
had done to them and said Joey was the only reason they lived through
it. I asked them to drop the charges against Joey and to stop shooting
at my house. They did that, and Joey went free.

Judy: What happened then? You still had to deal with Frank. And
by now, everyone in the house knows he's really dangerous.

Cheri: Yeah. And now he was back, living there again, and I was
really afraid of him. I had to do something and I didn't know what.
One evening, Frank and Joey borrowed my car to pick up their stolen
loot from a storage shed, but they never told me that. They parked
my car in front of the house and left to go to a bar together. I went
outside and saw the loot in my car. I used that as my reason. Now
I had an excuse to be angry.

Judy: I would think you already had an excuse. Plenty of excuses,
in fact.

Cheri: This was the excuse that would allow me to throw him
out. So I packed up Frank's stuff – also Joey's stuff, just to make it
look like I was mad at both of them - and I put it all outside. I had
taken Frank's shotgun apart while they were gone, and put it into
the closet, in pieces. I put Joey's loaded gun in there, too. I told Tony,
Bo and Heather to get out, in order to be safe. I loaded my .38 and
put it under my pillow.

Judy: You knew what you were doing was dangerous.

Cheri: Yes. They came home and went crazy when they saw their
stuff outside the house. Joey was calling me a fucking bitch and I
felt bad that I couldn't tell him what I was trying to do. Frank was
raging. *Raging.*

Judy: Were you alone with the kids?

Cheri: The kids were asleep in the back bedrooms. Bo and
Heather had refused to leave, said they wanted "to have my back."
They were in their bedroom closet, hiding. Tony was on the living
room couch, a blanket over his head, pretending to be asleep. Frank
stood up on the couch and walked on Tony, but he still refused to
come out from under the blanket. Joey got his loaded gun out of the

closet, where I'd put it, along with the parts to Frank's shotgun. We were all terrified. But when it came down to it, I was the only one really trying to deal with it. I felt like I was at fault because I had let Frank into our lives. This was my house, my kids, my friends, my responsibility.

From her essay, "Buried Secrets":
Frank was in a raging, psychotic frenzy. "You mother-fucking cunt, you think you're going to throw ME out? You owe me your sorry ass life, bitch!" He was screaming at me, spitting on me, describing how he was going to torture and kill me, my friends, and my children.

Judy: What was everyone else doing?
Cheri: Tony was on the couch, refusing to move. Joey was just looking down at the floor, his loaded 9mm in his hand, hanging at his side. Bo and Heather were hiding in the back. Frank ordered Tony to put his shotgun back together, so he did. I wanted to choke Tony for being such a coward. So now Frank had a loaded shotgun. He was shoving the shotgun into my face and spitting on me.
Judy: And what did you do?
Cheri: I tried to talk calmly to him. I knew that if I died, he would kill everyone else. He was not going to let anyone be a witness. I asked him if he believed in God. He said, "I am the Devil's brother." He told me he loves to kill people, that he would come in his pants when he did it. Nothing I said was working. He was crazed. He told me to get outside and get into the car. He went out to load up the car, thinking I would follow him. I ran into my bedroom. He came back inside and called out, "Where are you?" He thought I was going to call the cops. Now his voice was calm, which was scarier. He said he was going to kill me. Joey's voice changed, too, because he knew I had a gun back there. "She is NOT calling the cops, Frank!" He was trying to keep Frank from following me into the back room.

I looked at the phone but I knew it was too late for that. "God forgive me," kept running over and over in my head. "Shit, mother-fucker, can't you just leave?" I thought to myself. I almost buckled under the sadness of it.

As Cheri told this story to me, she began crying.

Cheri: Frank could have left. But he just had to walk through that fucking door. As soon as he came in, I just emptied the gun into him. I was a pretty good shot, but it wasn't hard. I fired my .38 special Smith and Wesson at arms' length. All the shots went into his chest. I was on auto pilot. I heard my dad talking to me: "Once you shoot someone, finish it. Make sure they can't get up." I took the barrel of the gun and beat his head with the butt of the gun. Everyone in the house heard the shots and they thought Frank was shooting me. I will never know if Joey would have sided with Frank if that had been true. I will never know.

My gun was empty when Joey ran in and emptied his nine milli-meter into Frank's dead body. My self-defense now looked like mangled road kill. Calling the police was now out of the question.

Judy: So, let me get this straight. Joey had his gun all along, but never thought to defend you against Frank? And he only shot him after Frank was dead on the floor?

Cheri: Yes. And now Joey has muddied the whole thing. I was going to call the police, explain that it was self-defense, but now we have bullets from two guns in the body. Joey had made a mess of the head. There was so much blood, hair, pieces of scalp, a fucking mess. So we decided to get rid of the body.

Judy: What about the kids?

Cheri: I went to their bedroom and reassured them that I was fine and that they should go back to sleep.

I asked Cheri's daughter and son if they could recall anything about that night.

Michelle: I think I have blocked out a lot of it. I was 10 years old, in the fourth grade. I knew something was going on. I knew it was bad. Jason was in his room, and I was in a bedroom closer to the living room. I remember hearing the fighting. Frank was yelling at Mom and I was really scared. I went into my brother's room. He was pretending to sleep. I stayed in his room that night.

Jason: I remember one gunshot, for some reason. After that, nothing. The next morning, my mom was excited, hyper – probably high as shit. I remember her saying, "Let's go shopping!"

Michelle: The next morning, they were pulling the rug up from the floor. We went shopping for cleaning supplies that day, like nothing had happened.

Judy: But you knew something had happened.

Michelle: I called my Dad soon after that. I said, "You need to come get us. We are not in a safe place." He didn't learn what had happened, the killing, until the cops came to interview me about what I knew a whole year later.

Cheri: Me and Heather and Bo had to clean up the mess. Nothing else was in order, so my house was going to be in order. We had to pick up pieces of his face, brain matter. Bo started heaving and was no help. You can never count on men, Judy. There was so much blood. I grabbed a tarp from the back yard and pulled Frank's body onto the tarp. Joey and Tony wrapped him up and put the body in the back of Tony's truck. They buried the body somewhere in the desert. Never told me where.

Judy: And the police never came looking for Frank?

Cheri: No. The police never came. But five years later, Bo was arrested for something and gave it up in exchange for leniency. That set off an investigation, but I was never charged.

Judy: Was the body ever found?

Cheri: No. We buried both the body and the secret.

I wish I could say I never used drugs again, that I never put myself, my children, or my friends in danger. Unfortunately, nothing could be further from the truth. I turned myself in and confessed to Frank's death in 1998 only because the police had arrested and charged Joey for it. Instead of arresting me, as I expected, they believed my story of self-defense and released both me and Joey. Not holding me accountable in some way was the worst thing they could have done. In my sick mind, killing became a justifiable option, and now the police had reinforced that delusion.

Judy: I'm curious. Did the killing of Frank Belize ever weigh on your conscience?

Cheri: I have never had one nightmare about it. It was a major psychological turning point for me. I was so relieved, I was giddy. I beat him. A guy who had struck terror in all of us. It was like a surge of power. It's very powerful to kill someone who was going to kill you.

Judy: Could you kill again?

Cheri: Yes, if I were protecting me and my family.

Chapter 15

Getting Away with Murder:
Lady Macbeth on Meth

I liked that TV show "How to Get Away With Murder." The difference is I never expected to get away with anything. I just didn't give a shit. What I was waiting for was to be punished. I could not seem to make that happen no matter what I did, so I continued to push the envelope, as they say. My extreme behavior escalated and surpassed any shit I had pulled before.

After Cheri killed Frank Belize, after her friends had buried the body in the desert, the fact that she had gotten away with shooting someone point blank in the chest five times, albeit in self-defense, was more corrosive than she could have anticipated. At first, she was "giddy" with the knowledge that she had been victorious over a homicidal psychopath. But getting away with it triggered a whole new set of emotions.

After I killed Frank, I remember meeting with everyone who was there (except the kids, of course). We were out in the backyard. Frank had stored a lot of shit in the shed which everyone except me distributed among themselves. I wanted nothing of Frank's and I sure as hell didn't want it on my property. I told everyone that if news of the killing ever came out, I would own it all. I just needed them to tell the truth about what happened. I believe that was our last conversation about the incident.

Bo and Heather moved on. Cheri lost track of Tony. She continued her tumultuous relationship with Joey, and they continued their joint love affair with meth. Still, in her own way, she seemed to be looking for ways to atone.

I would try to help people, I would take in abused animals. I used to pick up every hitchhiker and pull over every time I saw someone break down. I would even bring people home I'd never met before and get a tow truck for their car. I don't know if these were a direct result of the shame and guilt I felt about myself and my life, but I felt like I was at least doing something good for someone and I was a bit obsessed with it. I was obsessive-compulsive about keeping my house and yard clean.

Out, damned spot.

It wasn't long after that when Casey came into our lives. He was very young, very cute and likeable. More important, he was a cook.

Casey Lain has been Cheri's friend ever since he met her in 1993. He was living in Wrightwood, not far from Pinion Hills, and went in search of Cheri when he heard "about a chick who wanted to buy some meth." Casey told me that he was a full blown meth cook by the time he was 21.

"When you're the person who's doing that, you are like God. People bring you gifts, pies and this and that. NO one is more important than you. At the same time, everyone in the desert had guns and people were always trying to rob you."

Casey became fast friends with Cheri and Joey and was soon "part of their circle, a crazy spin cycle of the dope life." When I interviewed Casey over the phone, he said he had been sober for more than 19 years, had gotten his life together and was working in construction. But back in the 90's, he was completely caught up in the "complicated, explosive, poisonous, and dangerous" trade of cooking and dealing meth.

And like so many others who crossed paths with Cheri, Casey Lain was smitten.

"You don't meet many people like Cheri in your lifetime," he told me. "She has a certain aura about her, beautiful, tall, stunning. She overcomes everything. I saw her – on the one hand - as very feminine, a woman who was a great homemaker, taking care of children, sewing and cooking better than almost any woman I had met. On the other hand, she could do almost everything better than a man. I love Cheri. She was always true to her word, always had my back, and the way we lived out there in the desert, that was hard to find."

But for all her "feminine" skills, for all her honesty and empathy, added Casey, she was no pushover. "Yes, she was loyal to her friends. But I know one thing about Cheri. You don't fuck with Cheri."

Unfortunately, a few people tried to do just that, and Cheri's life became an impossible balancing act of trying to make a living in the meth business and trying to fend off the dangers that come with it, all while dealing with a boyfriend who proved, over and over again, that he was not reliable when trouble came knocking. Apparently, Joey's failure to protect her during the deadly confrontation with Frank Belize was not sufficient reason to end the relationship. Time and time again, he would bail on her when she needed him most. Time and time again, she would throw him out, then forgive him and take him back.

Joey and I would split up and get back together. I was crazy about him. He was adorable and funny, a great sense of humor. We had a great sexual relationship, best sex I ever had. But I know he didn't really feel the same for me. There were too many instances where he left me hanging out to dry. I couldn't stand the cowardice in him but I felt protective of him at the same time. He needed me, I thought, and I needed to be needed. I couldn't accept him as he was, but I kept taking him back.

Judy: It boggles the mind, this attachment to a guy who continually bails on you when the going gets tough.

Cheri: I was addicted to him. And co-dependent. You know, as in "I can fix him." And we were both on meth, don't forget. Years later, when I was studying drug addiction in prison, I learned that meth blocks activity in the frontal cortex of the brain, the area that deals with compassion and empathy and conscience. And you start operating from that more primitive part of the brain that focuses on survival. I needed meth to survive. We both did.

Joey and Casey hit it off immediately and Joey started his first cooking lessons. One day Joey comes in and tells me there is this rich dude [we will refer to him as "Darryl" in these pages, to protect his identity] who wants them to cook meth for him in San Dimas, a high-end area east of Los Angeles. He insisted I go with him, even though I didn't want to, since I had not learned how to cook yet. I thought it was strange, but he cajoled me into it. We head out to San Dimas and arrive at this beautiful home in a lovely neighborhood. We are sitting at the dining room table when in walks Darryl. I was blown away. He was tall, dark and handsome and I was smitten right away. After we met, he took us to his family's ranch not far from the house.

I have been a horse lover all my life, so the fact he owned horses just added to his allure. He had a quarter horse filly in a paddock, but when he tried to show her off, the horse wouldn't let him catch her. I ducked under the fence to help him and the filly just walked right up to me and shoved her nose in my hand. I was surprised, Darryl was impressed, and I think the connection between us started at that moment.

Darryl had paid us a sizeable amount to establish a meth operation in the ranch house. Joey had the cook set up on the kitchen floor, but it was not going well. Joey simply did not know enough, at that point, to do the job. Late that night, I woke up and went into the kitchen. Darryl asked me to finish the cook and I laughed. I told him I had no idea how to cook and he looked at me in surprise. Darryl had been told there was this "beautiful redhead who cooked in the desert," so when I appeared with Joey, David assumed I was the actual cook.

Cheri was furious with Joey for setting up this bait-and-switch scam in an effort to get some easy money upfront. She broke up with Joey. Again.

I was not into ripping people off and it looked as though I was one of the guilty party. I tried to learn how to cook – at least enough to make it right – and went back to Darryl's. He set up the cook in a huge warehouse where his dad had an amazing yacht stored. I completely botched it. There was smoke from the cook rolling out everywhere. We ran outside and did our best to fan the smoke, but it was useless. I am amazed no one called the fire department. There was significant damage to the yacht and the building. I was devastated and embarrassed. Darryl, on the other hand, was calm and forgiving. Amazing.

Darryl had two lovely daughters and a beautiful ex-wife. We did sleep together but his heart was elsewhere and we remained fast friends. He even helped me rip the carpet out of the house in Pinion Hills and replace the wood flooring where Frank had died. Later, I got back together with Joey and that infuriated him, so we didn't talk for a while. Darryl learned how to cook meth for himself and became quite good at it.

If he ever reads this, I want him to know that he has always been someone I love and appreciate.

Cheri's life, by this time, was entirely driven by dealing and consuming meth. In the high desert of California, police were not a huge presence, but now and then they would make an appearance and threaten to interfere with the growing meth business around Pinion Hills. One night, when Cheri came home after being away for a couple of days visiting a friend, she pulled in to find cop cars waiting for her in the driveway.

They put me against the car and handcuffed me immediately. They said I was under arrest for a stolen motorcycle. A friend had given me a nice little Ninja, which was in the garage. Thank God I had already filed the paperwork with the DMV and I told the cops I had the information inside the house. Then I saw Davey, Joey's older brother, in one of the cop cars.

Casey Lain was no fan of Joey's brother. "That dude," he told me, "was a real piece of work. A lying, cheating, stealing rat. Back then, there were a lot of lying meth addicts around. But there was no snitching, ever."

Apparently, Joey's brother Davey didn't get the memo. Cheri thought it was suspicious that Davey was in one of the police cars, but at that moment, she was more worried about what they would find inside her house.

The cops bring me in the house. They go to my bedroom, where the window is wide open and a bag of meth is lying on the floor and there is a meth pipe on my dresser. I know I am going to jail at this point. My gun stash is under my waterbed and they pull all of them out and lay them on the bed. None of them is registered to me.

Cheri had good reason to think she was about to be arrested. The meth and the guns were bad enough, but when she opened a desk drawer to pull out the paperwork on the motorcycle, there was a big bag of pot inside the drawer.

A trifecta of trouble.

I feel numb inside, just accepting the fact that I am screwed.

Cheri then phoned the friend who gave her the motorcycle, who confirmed that it was a gift and not stolen. So at least she had cleared up that issue. But the police were clearly after something else. They asked her about the people who jumped out of the bedroom window when they pulled up. She said "I don't have a clue. I have been gone for a couple of days." She knew, however, that one of those people had to be Joey.

Then something astonishing happened. Instead of taking her to jail, the cops took her handcuffs off and said she and Davey would be released.

I cannot fucking believe it. They should have taken me straight to jail. When they go to take Davey's handcuffs off, they say the key won't work and ask if I have any bolt cutters, and I say that I probably have a pair in the tool shed. One of the cops follows me to the back yard with his flashlight. Now mind you, I have no outside lights whatsoever. It is pitch black. So it's quite a shock for me when we walk in the shed and find a full blown lab. The flask is in the middle of the floor with a finished cook in it, and plates of ephedrine are on the counter. My heart stopped. All I could say was, "Well, I guess I don't have any bolt cutters."

We go back into the kitchen. Nothing to say, nothing to do but wait for the handcuffs to go back on. I look over at Davey and see that his handcuffs are already off. I realized the bolt cutter request was just a cover. So it's clear that Davey had spilled his guts about this lab in the back shed but, at least, he also told them I knew nothing about it because I had been away for a couple of days. They had put me through the test and I had passed.

The cops say they are leaving and I am beyond dumbfounded. I am both terrified and raging at the same time. I told Davey that we were going to get everything out of that shed and throw it over the fence. Fast. I turn the hose on to wash everything down, I have my shotgun and I am screaming about killing Joey. We are throwing shit over the fence when Michael Larson [a neighbor] shows up at my back gate. He had been there with Joey and Davey during the cook and he had come back to get his dirt bike. I screamed at him to get the fuck off my property but he insisted on getting his bike. I never before had made such a perfect one-handed shot. I shot a round of buckshot at his feet and he leaped up in the air and pirouetted like a bloated ballerina. The buckshot got him in the ass. He took off running and I walked back in the house with the shotgun. As I walked through the back door, the cops were coming back in through the front door. They had never really left.

One of them said, "I just received a report of shots fired."

I said, "Yeah, that was me. I just shot Michael Larson in the ass."

"Why?"

"Because he didn't get off my property soon enough."

"Where is he now?"

"I don't know, but I heard his feet flapping across the desert."

Both cops laughed. Michael Larson was known to them, and not in a good way. The female cop picked up the shotgun, emptied the rest of the bullets, and set the gun on the counter.

"Cheri," she said, laughing, "Please don't shoot anyone else tonight. We have enough paperwork because of you."

And then they left. That was it. That was all.

That was when I decided to become a cook.

Chapter 16

The Red-Headed Cook of the Desert

"I did it for me. I liked it. I was good at it. And, I was really...I was alive."
—*Walter White*

According to Cheri's longtime friend, Casey Lain, "Crazy Cheri is a legend out here in the California desert to this day." Hyperbole, perhaps, but many years after she reportedly earned that reputation, including those long years spent in prison, a member of a California Parole Board would remark, "God. You're almost like somebody out of *Breaking Bad*. Have you seen that?"

Judy: Had you even heard of *Breaking Bad*?

Cheri: I had never watched it, of course, because I was in prison when I heard that. So when I finally got out, I watched it.

Judy: And?

Cheri: I didn't really get the comparison. I mean, I never put dead bodies in tubs of acid. And my meth labs were in trailers and kitchens. Walter White set up a huge factory operation.

Judy: Details aside, I imagine the parole board's comparison was meant to describe the bigger picture.

The bigger picture at this point of her story, in 1993, was all-meth, all the time. And there's one big difference between Walter White and Cheri Mathews. He cooked, but he never used.

I was tweaking, I was crazy. The kids were with their father, because I got worse and worse. I felt so guilty, and I called less and less. I could never sit still and think. I was addicted, so cooking was the best way to take care of my own habit and make enough money to support myself. The whole process of cooking is addictive.

Learning to cook methamphetamine was a source of pride for Cheri. Casey taught her the basics, but she liked the idea that she was not just a cook, but a chemist. Without going into a detailed "how-to" lesson here, the method for producing the drug is basically four-steps. First, combine ephedrine with ammonia and lithium, or iodine and phosphorous. Add water. Add a solvent like gasoline, and extract the methamphetamine. And last, heat the mixture by using acid or some other substance to crystallize the product. That whole process, "the cook," can be quite dangerous, especially during the heating. Many of the substances used are flammable or corrosive. The waste materials from the cook are also highly unstable. Meth cooks perform a balancing act, constantly measuring something called "PH" factor, a test of whether their formula is too acidic or too alkaline. If the PH number is off, the results can be disastrous.

Some cooks use what's called an "instant meth approach," a sort of "shake and bake" process. The ingredients are combined in a plastic or glass container and then shaken and heated. The meth is then extracted. This process can also be very hazardous, as the substance in the containers are very volatile and can explode. And, of course, they sometimes do, sometimes wreaking a considerable amount of damage, injury and even death.

The desert provides the space and ventilation and isolation required for a good "cook." Meth labs require various appliances, including pots, pans, flasks and stoves with burners, as well as hoses for ventilation and curtains to block people on the outside from seeing what's going on inside.

In addition to the risks of explosions, *using* meth involves potential cutting agents that can be toxic, resulting in "meth mouth" (rotting teeth), weight loss and organ damage.

Pharmacies have cracked down on people buying suspicious quantities of some of these ingredients. For example, purchases of ephedrine (found in medications such as Sudafed) are now carefully monitored. Back in Cheri's meth-cooking days, she employed a sophisticated cadre of "runners" who would go to separate stores and buy only one ingredient at a time. They would have to show their drivers' licenses, so their errands were disparate and changeable.

I fancied myself an up and coming chemist. The truth was I really didn't know shit. But I got lucky sometimes and my meth came out great.

Cheri bought 10 acres of land on the top of a mountain near Lake Isabella. She paid for a stolen motorhome with two pounds of meth, drove it up the switchbacks to her land and paid someone to haul her travel trailer up there, as well. When she was cooking, she left the house in Pinion Hills and stayed in that motorhome. The meth lab was in the trailer. She had lots of customers, including members of the Orange County Chapter of the Hells Angels.

I had different people pick up my ephedrine, phosphorus, iodine crystals, and glassware. I was in heaven. The property was beautiful, 7000 feet up and no neighbors. I could go up there for a month, just me and my dog. I thought I had found my place in this world. I was so delusional that I wanted to pass it on to my children.

Now how sick is that?

Cheri used other sites for cooking, as well, when the opportunity came along, and when she wanted to cook closer to home. Sometimes those opportunities backfired.

I had a good friend, Tommy, who managed an old tungsten mine no longer in use. He told Joey and me that we could cook there. There was a huge lab and we got to work. We had everything going. Tommy had gone to town, but Joey was still with me when we heard someone drive in. Joey told me he would waylay the guy outside, but instead he got in his car and left. I had the lab door locked and I was completely terrified. There was no way to stop the cook. Nowhere I could go. There was only one door in and out. I heard Joey drive away. I prayed that whoever it is, they didn't have a key. The guy started banging on the door and then I heard a key turn in the lock.

I decided to play deaf. I turned my back on the door and acted like I didn't have a clue. The guy was yelling at me. I just continued to swirl the flasks, like I couldn't hear him. He finally touched me and I jumped, turned around and started talking to him in totally phony sign language. He fell for it. In fact, he was super apologetic. I smiled and wrote him a note saying I was just doing what I was told to do. He asked me where Tommy was and I wrote him a note saying Tommy went to town. I kept cooking like it's the thing to do. He left. I was about to shit my pants.

Joey showed up later to get me. Tommy got fired from his manager job. Not because the owner realized that we had a meth lab there. He thought Tommy was trying to pull gold from the tungsten on the property by using mercury, which is highly volatile. He had no idea what we were actually doing. I had pulled it off, but at the cost of Tommy's job. And once again, Joey had left me hanging in the wind.

Close calls like this did nothing to deter Cheri from her chosen line of work. Not even the time that a flask exploded in her face.

I was cooking in the trailer in my backyard this time. The sun was coming up and I was tired. There was still some mixture stuck to the side of the flask, so I touched it with the blowtorch to hurry it up. I knew better, but I was tired and did not want to listen to the warning voice in my head screaming "No!" The blast blew me backward against the wall. I was blinded, but I thought what I was "seeing" was fire. I ran towards the house to get the hose, tripping over big cement planters on the back patio. I hit that sonofabitch at a full run and flew into the air and landed on my back. I got up and finally reached the hose and was running back with it when, no shit, I tripped over the same planter. My shins and knees were screaming but I kept running with the hose. It wasn't long enough, and when it ran out, I almost yanked my arm out of its socket and down I went. I somehow managed to feel my way back to the house and the phone. Feeling the buttons, I called my neighbor Cathy.

She came over and I was screaming at her to put out the fire.

"There is no fire, Cheri." She was horrified because it looked as though someone had shot me in the head. I had a big hole in the center of my forehead.

Then it hit me.

"I'm blind, Cathy!"

The fire was in my eyes.

Cathy took Cheri to the emergency room at St. Mary's Hospital in Apple Valley. She still couldn't feel or see anything. The glass was in her face and eyes and she was covered in blood.

Cathy said, "Everyone is staring at you. I'm so sorry, Cheri, but you look like Frankenstein." I told Cathy that when they examined me, they would probably put procaine in my eyes for the pain. "Watch where they put it," I told her, "and steal as much as you can. This is going to be bad and I'm going to need it." They took me in to the examining room and the doctor asked what had happened. I told him a bottle of something blew up. He doused my eyes with procaine (from a previous eye injury I knew this drug would bring instant pain relief) and left the room. Cathy snatched up two bottles for me.

The doctor had gone to call the cops. So there I was, being questioned by those guys. I ran a bullshit story that probably no one believed, but they felt sorry for me so they left it alone.

St. Mary's couldn't help me, so they suggested I go to Loma Linda University Hospital. Did I go there right away? Of course not. I had the eye drops to tide me over so I could go back to my house and hide everything. I was worried, because the cops had my name and I figured they could show up at any time.

After making sure all signs of a meth cooking operation were cleaned up, Cheri finally got to Loma Linda.

The difference was night and day. The first thing I asked them was, "Are you going to call the cops on me?" They said, "No. We want to save your eyes." They had never had a case like mine and the medical students were giddy with excitement. I told them exactly what was in my eyes. They did some sort of test and said, "Zero pressure and zero PH. Total blindness."

I had figured that out by now. So when they told me they were going to try something new, I said "Go for it. I've got nothing to lose."

Cheri had surgery, the glass was removed from her eyes, her eyeballs were stitched back in place (a rather rudimentary way of describing a complicated procedure), and the pressure was restored. They gave her drops to neutralize the acid.

They gave me several different drops to put in every so many hours. When I woke up in the recovery room, Joey was there with flowers for me. My eyes had to stay bandaged for a certain amount of time and Joey faithfully gave me my eye drops every four hours. Eventually, they replaced the bandages with these weird round discs with little pinholes in them. My retina in one eye was in danger of detaching, but these discs helped me see. I had the worst migraines of my life. Too much "seeing" caused a pain so terrible that all I could do was lay still and try not to cry.

They saved my eyes. It was a fucking miracle.

A doctor I saw at The Eye Institute cracked up when I told him they had "PH-d my eyes like I PH my dope." He also warned me about putting too much pressure on my eyes. "Can I still go bungee jumping? I really love bungee jumping." None of that, he said, for quite a while.

Perhaps the doctor just assumed she would give up cooking meth as well as bungee jumping, considering that she had come perilously close to blindness.

My eyes were blood red, but they healed eventually. Did I stop cooking? Hell no. But I did wear protective glasses when I remembered to do it, which was not often.

Not long after that, I planned on seeing my son Jason for his 12th birthday, but Joey let me down, again, and failed to show up to drive me to Nevada. So I got on a plane. Not a great idea. My eyes felt like they were bursting. The blood vessels were bursting. I had blood running down my face, but there was nothing to do but wait it out. I hid my face and when the plane landed, I felt my way through the exit tunnel to the place where my sister Susie was to pick me up. I told her I couldn't see. I didn't want the kids to know, so I wore dark glasses while I was at their house.

For those wondering how in the world a woman who almost went blind while cooking meth would return to that way of life, with all the dangers attached (exploding meth labs being only one possibility), I can only refer you back to Chapter 7, "Cunning, Baffling, and Powerful." After a refresher course in the insanity of addiction, you may still ask yourself, "What will it take?" But at least you will know that whatever it takes, Cheri's long slide down into complete demoralization is not there yet. Not even close.

Chapter 17

When Pogonips Collide

Fallon, Nevada is ground zero for Cheri's family. In 1994, various family members arrived there at the same time, each with a different motivation for their journey. Cheri's sister Susie came to Fallon because she had a court date to deal with her divorce and child custody issues. Their half-brother Ronnie came to testify. Casey Lain came because he was, at that time, in a relationship with Susie. Cheri's youngest sister, Mandy, came because Susie had asked her to be there to provide emotional support during her divorce hearing.

Mandy: When I was 19, I was so out of touch with my sisters that I didn't even tell them I got married. I had a pager with a 1-800 number so that they could get hold of me, if they had to. Susie called me and said she was in a custody fight and wanted me to come to Fallon, Nevada. I was still using drugs at the time, living in California. I arrived in Fallon, where Susie had a motel room. Brother Ronnie came over and was smoking meth in the room. I had never smoked meth, just snorted it. The next day, I didn't feel well, so I didn't go to court with Susie.

Casey: I had gone fishing, and when I got back to the motel room, I threw the brother out. Didn't like him, didn't trust him. That night, after Susie had returned from testifying in court, cops

raided the motel room and found an ounce of speed in a tampon box.

Mandy: Apparently, Susie and Ronnie had both talked about drug use when testifying in court. So we were all arrested. I ended up in a jail cell with Susie. The next day, Cheri came to town.

Cheri: I didn't know about any of this. I was coming to Fallon for two reasons: I wanted to see Jason for his 13th birthday and give him the dirt bike he wanted; and I had an appointment with a lawyer to see if I could fight Jerry's effort to take away my visitation rights with my kids. A judge had ruled that I could only visit them with a chaperone present because of my lifestyle.

Judy: So you had no idea that Casey and your two sisters were in jail?

Cheri: No. I parked and went into the lawyer's office. Even though I had mailed him a check as a retainer, he said he was declining the case, and he handed my money back. I was really upset. Why couldn't he tell me he didn't want to take the case over the phone? I left to go to the bank to deposit the money. When I walked outside, I was surrounded by cops. They were waiting for me. That outstanding warrant had caught up with me.

Judy: So they were clearly tipped off that you were coming.

Cheri: Yes. And what made it worse was that when they searched my car, they found meth and a .357 magnum under the seat.

Mandy remembers the moment Cheri was led to the cell where she and Susie were being held.

Mandy: So now, all three sisters are in the same jail, which the guards thought was hilarious. Cheri wasn't laughing. She beat the hell out of Susie in the cell. The guards looked the other way.

Cheri was furious with Susie for a couple of reasons. She had earlier given Susie money to pay for a lawyer for this custody hearing, but found out that Susie had bought meth with it instead. And she was furious because Susie had pulled Mandy into her mess. Mandy, Susie and Casey all made bail and were released with court dates. Cheri, on the other hand, was given a three month sentence on the outstanding warrant.

Judy: So who set up whom?

Cheri: I'm not sure. I think both Susie and Ronnie had mouthed off about drug use in the family while they were testifying, so that didn't help.

Judy: Casey told me that he thinks Ronnie ratted them all out for a promise of a reduced sentence.

Cheri: Could be. I don't know. I would really like to know how the cops were tipped off that I was in town and were ready to grab me the moment I left the lawyer's office.

Judy: Perhaps the lawyer looked up your record, saw the outstanding warrant and decided not to take your case? On the other hand, if he tipped off the cops, that would be a violation of professional ethics.

Cheri: I don't think I will ever know. All I know is they were waiting outside his office.

I was unable to ask the lawyer in question, because Cheri couldn't remember his name. And I would have asked her half-brother Ronnie if he had made a deal with the police, but Ronnie died of a drug overdose some years ago. So did her other half-brother, Kevin (if you have trouble following the bewildering parade of siblings and half-siblings, keep in mind that Cheri's mother married six times). If anyone doubts that drug addiction is a family disease, they need look no further than this particular family tree to see the boughs crashing to the ground from the weight of it.

Cheri was released after serving just two months of the three month sentence in the Fallon jail.

Cheri: I went on a hunger strike. It made the newspaper and they wanted to get rid of me. They reduced the charges to simple possession of drugs and set a court date. A friend in California put up the bail money and I went back to Pinion Hills.

Judy: And did you go back to Nevada for that court date?

Cheri: I don't know why, but I did. I was crying so hard when I left California because I had a feeling I wasn't coming back. Joey told me to knock it off. He was sure I was going to get probation. It was my first offense, he said. And he promised he would see me when I got back.

Judy: Did you get probation?

Cheri: No. I was sentenced to three years in the Nevada state prison in Carson City. I wasn't prepared for that. The judge knew about my background. "This is more than a possession charge," he said, "and you know it."

I never saw Joey, my home, or my belongings again.

The two months she had served in the Fallon jail was her first experience with incarceration. The three year sentence in Carson City was a whole new world. And not in a good way.

I remember sitting on the prison yard in Carson City and realizing that there was something so wrong with me that I wasn't worth loving. I became convinced of it and I became very bitter and angry. While I was there, Joey got a girl pregnant and married her. He packed up my house and put everything in storage. The house was repossessed. Everything in storage disappeared, was sold or given away. All that I ever salvaged were my photo albums.

Michelle was in 6th grade when her Mom was sentenced to prison in Carson City. "What was really weird was that my DARE teacher at school was one of the cops who arrested my mom," she told me. DARE, the Drug Awareness and Resistance Education program, aims to educate kids about the dangers of drugs at an early age. "My DARE speech was the runner up to the winner who gave the DARE graduation speech," Michelle told me. She was, of course, sad that her mom was in prison. "My dad took us to visit her there. Dad and her started flirting and I was really mad. I did not want them back together again. They were not good for each other."

It occurred to me that for children like Michelle and her brother Jason, a DARE program would be incredibly superfluous.

Losing almost everything, from her boyfriend to her house to all her possessions, Cheri might have experienced the utter demoralization that leads addicts to surrender, to ask for help, to begin the hard work of climbing back from the abyss.

But this was not that time. Not yet.

Cheri: I lost my mind during that time. I had no coping skills at all. None. Joey had abandoned me and my house had been repossessed. I lived by a certain code and I expected others to live by it, too. Loyalty, honesty, no snitching, all that. I was just so, so angry, feeling powerless to do anything about what was going on outside. And nobody from the outside - not Joey, not my mother – came to "rescue" me.

Judy: How did you get through it?

Cheri: They sent me to fire camp and initially it was great because I was learning something, fighting fires and doing road crew work. But that didn't last long because I got into a fight with a White girl and her Black girlfriend. They were walking down the hallway and we were supposed to get out of their way, stand back while they passed. But I refused and walked right between them. The White girl said, in a nasty voice, "Excuse me?" And I responded, "No, excuse ME" and grabbed her by the throat. We started fighting and all the Black inmates who were there joined in. They got my arms pinned behind my back, and slammed my face into a metal bunk. My face just exploded. I was screaming and the guards finally intervened. My face was a bloody mess, my eyes were swollen shut. The guards took me back to the main prison again in Carson City.

Judy: That sounds like a punishment.

Cheri: They blamed me for starting a riot. They were right. I *had* started it. I was the bad guy, Judy. No excuses. And they put me in the hole.

Judy: Solitary confinement?

Cheri: Yes. For several months. I worked out in the cell and in the exercise yard to keep in shape. I read a lot. I liked Stephen King novels. And I really like being alone, so it wasn't as bad as you might

think. But Black inmates were threatening to kill me when I got out, yelling at me for the whole hour each day I was in the exercise yard.

Judy: What happened when you went back into the main prison?

Cheri: I thought they were going to kill me. The leader of their group approached me in the yard and my insides were shaking. Then she said, "I just want to shake your hand. I heard you got into a fight with a white girl, but got jumped and put up one hell of a fight!" I couldn't believe it. And then I was sent back to fire camp.

Judy: So at least you were back to working outside.

Cheri: Not for long. They brought me back to the prison and put me in solitary again. Authorities in California still had an open file on the Frank Belize case and they came to Nevada to question me. Bo, one of the guys who was at the house when I killed Frank, got busted for drugs and gave up the story to get leniency. I refused to talk, even to give my name when they turned on the tape recorder. But it was still considered an open case and it would come back to haunt me later. And the worst part was that they interviewed the kids as well.

Jerry was living in Fallon with Michelle and Jason and his second wife, Kim. Jerry had given up alcohol and drugs and was attending AA meetings.

Michelle: My dad was a good dad. I went to AA meetings with him, and I would eat doughnuts there.

Jerry: I knew nothing about the Frank Belize case because the kids had never told me. They had apparently been sworn to secrecy. So when two San Bernardino detectives showed up to talk to me and the kids about this open murder case, I couldn't imagine where this was going. It certainly didn't help my marriage with Kim. I was blindsided.

Michelle: I was ten years old, in the 4th grade, when Frank was murdered. I had blocked most of it out of my mind. The detectives interviewed me when I was in the 5th grade. I told them I couldn't remember much. I did remember that Frank was scary.

Jason: I couldn't remember enough to tell the cops anything. I was able to identify Frank's photo, but not because I remembered his face. I remembered his chest. His nipples were pierced, with skull earrings dangling from them. That's how I knew the photo was him.

The detectives flew back to California and the kids were never asked about it again. Meanwhile, Cheri's prison experience was more of a lesson in revenge than remorse.

Cheri: I had no ability to look at my part in anything. I was always the victim. Taking responsibility for the things I had done would not come until much, much later. At that time, my head was not right. I could not let go of what had happened to me in California – Joey's betrayal, my missing things. Who had them? Carson City was a bad experience, although I did care about one person, my cellmate.

Judy: Tell me about her.

Cheri: Marnie Peot. She was serving multiple life sentences for two or three murders. I was just serving three years for possession, and knew I was getting out. We really hit it off and she became my best friend. I used to write to her after I got out. She is still there, will never get out. (Long pause) She lost her mind in there.

[Note: Marnie Peot died in her cell in 2017 after a fight with another inmate. Cheri had not heard the news until I told her about finding a news article with details of her death.]

The parole board agreed to grant Cheri parole after she had served 16 months of the three year sentence. It was a close call, though, since she had a couple of black marks – one from the riot at fire camp and one from the open murder case. When she was released, she was picked up at the prison by her mom, Carole, and her two kids.

Cheri: I went to Fallon to live with my mom. I was glad the kids were with Jerry. He had straightened out his life. I should have been grateful that I was out of prison, that I had this opportunity to begin a new life.

Judy: Sounds familiar.

Cheri: I got a job "flagging" for a construction company, and I got to see my kids. But I also got back on meth. People lose everything behind meth. It's insanity. There is no right thinking, no clear decision-making. It's just primal. No conscience, all selfishness, deprivation of everything good. You lose your soul.

Michelle: When she got out of prison, the first time, she was living at my grandma's and working at a flagging job at a construction site. I have a bad memory of one time when she was supposed to pick me up from the skating rink. She showed up drunk. I didn't know how to drive. I was in junior high school, 7th grade. And it was a stick shift. But I had to try. She was shit-faced. So I drove home, in fits and starts. (Pause) It was terrible. And terrifying.

Cheri disappointed her kids on a fairly regular basis, especially on their birthdays. On Jason's 12th birthday, you may recall, she arrived from the airport wearing dark glasses to hide her bleeding eyes, the injury caused by that meth lab explosion and exacerbated by the air pressure on the plane. On Jason's 13th birthday, she arrived in Fallon to give him a dirt bike, only to be arrested and held for two months in the Fallon jail. Michelle was also let down on numerous occasions.

Michelle: I remember being excited about Mom coming for my birthday, then she wouldn't come. I gave up hoping. But when she would come, it was like she hung the sun. I was always so excited about seeing her. But it was also chaos. A shit show. Because Dad was unhappy seeing her and always had a hard time with it.

Jerry Mathews' marriage to Kim did not last long. But he married for a third time, to a 6th grade teacher named Becky, and that had staying power, despite the strains of combining two families. Becky Mathews spoke with me on the phone about the emotional roller coaster endured by Michelle and Jason.

Becky: Their birthdays. It was really tough to watch. Cheri would promise to be there, but wouldn't show up. It was devastating to them. Later, when Cheri was in prison, the kids would sometimes refuse to write her letters. So I wrote to her and let her know what the kids were doing. And since they already had experienced being left by two mothers, first Cheri and then Kim, I had to constantly reassure them I wasn't going anywhere.

Judy: And were you able to reassure them?

Becky: Michelle related to me better than Jason. I remember I said something negative once about Cheri, and Jason came unglued. "Never talk about my mom like that!" Michelle, however, would say things like "You're so good for my dad, because you are so natural." I could never get her to explain that. Did she mean I was down to earth, more like a typical mom? That I didn't gamble or do drugs? I never knew.

Jerry: It was hard for Becky. She was a really good stepmom. She would watch all those times when Cheri would try hard, mean well, but it wouldn't go well. Those times Cheri promised the kids she would be there to see them and failed to show. Once she gambled away all her money before she got there. It happened so many times. I hated to see their hearts broken over and over.

One might think that this on-again, off-again approach to motherhood would have soured the kids on Cheri for good. But while that bond would be strained to a near-breaking point at various times over the years, the bond would never be severed entirely. And in 1997, after Cheri was released from prison in Carson City, she made one more desperate attempt to bring her kids to live with her. Desperate, and doomed to fail.

Chapter 18

Are We There Yet?

In a word, no. But you knew that already. Cheri has many, many hard miles to go before she sleeps, or – in this case – before she wakes up. Her ability, however, to stay *physically* awake for days on end continues to be fueled by her meth addiction. No longer cooking, at this point, but still using, chasing that life of never-enough. Add alcohol to the mix, shake well, and you have a literal recipe for disaster. The relapse came swiftly, despite her many months of hard time in the state prison in Nevada, despite being given yet another "second chance," this time with an early parole that sends her home to Fallon to live with her mother, Carole, and near her kids.

Cheri was so far from "woke," so far from hitting her bottom, as they say in recovery circles, that her description of what comes next is hard to square with the woman who today is recounting her story. And *that* woman - vibrant, funny, empathic, honest - who now shares these darkest moments from her past, is why I keep listening. The 38-year-old woman she is describing bears almost no resemblance to the 60-year-old Cheri I know. The woman she is describing is not, to be blunt, someone I would want to know. So hang on. This is where things get really dark.

I'm back in Nevada, on parole. My mom has a cast on her leg which went to the top of her thigh from a broken femur, a break she received from a horse kick. She is hooked on Vicodin and her life is pretty messed up. She's gambled thousands of dollars and cleaned out Doug [her fifth husband] for all he had. He leaves her, which is too bad, because he was a great guy. She then married a Mexican horse wrangler named Honorato. He was 23 years old. He later died in a truck accident.

I think it's fair to say that Cheri's mom, the one who abandoned her at age three, is not going to provide the secure home the parole board may have envisioned. Perhaps it would not have mattered, anyway, since Cheri was set on finding Joey and making him "explain himself."

Cheri: I never saw him again, after he abandoned me in prison and married someone else. But I was obsessed with him. He had taken everything from me. I am really a crazy person now.

She returned to California, a violation of her Nevada parole, and found her old friend "Darryl."

He got me an old motorhome and gave me some meth and money, and told me to get back to Nevada and take care of my parole while I lived in the motorhome. I took off but as I was driving down Highway 134 towards Palmdale, the wiring on the motorhome fried and the lights went out. I knew a couple who lived nearby in the hills near Llano, so I went there and stayed with them. I was so depressed and just wanted to give up. But I had plenty of dope so I could share it with my friends and still sell enough to buy groceries.

That's when I met David Hepburn. Davey. He was their friend and he came to look at my motorhome to see if it could be fixed. Then he started coming over every day to spend time with me. We would talk late into the night. He was a good listener.

He was also very dangerous. But she didn't know that yet.

Davey told me that he supplied the Mexican mafia with vacant properties to cook on and said he could get me what I would need to start cooking again. He took me to his place. It was a disaster. The cabin was filthy and most of the rooms had no furniture. Concrete floors, no rugs or curtains. It wasn't livable to me.

Not livable. The reasonable reaction, you might think, would be to leave. Immediately. As in, run for your life. But no. Cheri's reaction was just the opposite.

I had found somewhere I could live and be needed. Davey wasn't good looking, so it wasn't that. He had been burned badly and was scarred over much of his body. It made me want to take care of him that much more.

Cheri: In the beginning, Davey was on the same page. We worked together to fix up the place, a cabin on five acres of land in Llano. We built new kitchen cabinets, repaired anything that needed fixing.

Judy: So he owned this place?

Cheri: No. He said he was renting it. But he never paid rent, so he was really squatting on the land. But I didn't want to know. I just wanted to have a home that would be nice enough to convince Jerry to let the kids visit and stay for a while. I convinced myself I was in love with him. As long as I was helping, Davey and I got along just fine. But as the place started to come together, things started changing.

When I would return from a trip to the store, he would accuse me of being somewhere else. He would make me show him the receipts from the grocery store to prove that no extra time had elapsed. He would count my change to make sure I hadn't kept any money. I was not allowed to have money of my own. Obviously, these accusations would upset me, and I would leave to stay with friends. But I always came back. I went back because I had nowhere to go, and I was determined to make it work, never to be homeless. It was another insane, controlling relationship. Once again, I thought I could fix things.

Cheri: I know it makes no sense, but I was getting sicker and sicker. I was so tweaked out, so insane. When I finished working on the house, I became obsessed with looking for pretty rocks to collect in the desert. I would do this all day long. Davey got me into it. I was so beaten down, so sick. It wasn't me anymore. It was the shell of me.

Judy: Did he physically abuse you?

Cheri: No. The abuse was psychological, emotional, financial. And it built up over time. He was growing more and more paranoid, and both of us were using meth every day. He would clear the dirt around the cabin with a drag [a rake-like attachment for the rear of a truck] so he could see if anyone had walked on the property. He had promised me that he would set me up with materials to cook with, but he never did. Instead, he controlled everything I did.

Judy: Such as?

Cheri: If I tried to leave, he would chase me down with his big Chevy truck through the desert, spinning circles around me like an animal. Then he would turn around and say, "Hi, sweetheart, look at all I'm doing for you." Like it never happened. His whole personality would change. He was so crazy he didn't know what he was doing. And I felt sorry for him.

Judy: Why didn't you leave the moment you had a chance?

Cheri: I was getting more and more insane myself. And if I threatened to leave, he would tell me he would let all our animals starve to death if I took off. It was his way of controlling me, because he knew I would never let the horses and dogs go hungry. And I knew he would make good on that threat.

Judy: Did you have any idea about this side of him? Weren't there any signs or warnings?

Cheri: Yeah. Quite a few. A woman named Rose arrived one day, accompanied by two big guys carrying guns. Turns out she had been Davey's girlfriend before me, and she had been driven away without any of her belongings. The only way she felt safe enough to retrieve her stuff was with two armed guys by her side.

Judy: And that didn't worry you?

Cheri: It did. Because I could imagine the day when I might be in the same situation. Also, a woman in the area told me that Davey had an ex-wife and six kids who were hiding from him in Los Angeles. She said that when they lived with him, she used to sneak food to the wife and kids when she could. "Get away from him," she told me.

Judy: And yet, you stayed.

Cheri: Behind all of it, I still thought he loved me and that I could make him better and that I could create a home where my kids could come visit. And finally, they did come.

Jerry let me have the kids for one month in the summer. Michelle was about 14 and Jason was 11. I asked Jerry to meet me in Bishop, where we would pick up the kids.

Jerry Mathews remembers this time vividly. "When we dropped the kids off in Bishop, I did not get good vibes from that guy. I mean, there was a bad aura about him. A bad, bad feeling, the kind that makes your hair stand up on your head. He didn't say anything, never smiled. The kids got in their car and they drove away."

Michelle remembers it vividly, as well.

Michelle: I had packed a lot of stuff, including a suitcase of shoes. I was a teenager! And we thought we would be staying for a month. I remember being really scared of Davey. He was crazy. He photographed our shoe prints so he could match them against footprints in the dirt around the house to make sure no strangers were coming around.

(Long pause)

I had never seen my mom scared of anyone in my life. And the moment I got there, I saw the fear. Seeing my mom scared, scared me.

Davey was not friendly to the kids. It was obvious he didn't want them there. He wouldn't allow us to run the swamp cooler in the blistering heat. He would pretend to be nice to them and then turn around and become downright evil. For example, he would ask Jason if he wanted to ride on his motorcycle, then as Jason was getting ready to get on for a ride, Davey would say, "What the fuck do you think you're doing?" My daughter said, "I have never seen you controlled like this, Mom. We have to get away from here."

"Becky and I got a call from Michelle," remembers Jerry. " 'Daddy,' she told me, 'we don't feel okay here.' And she told me about their footprints, how this guy was paranoid."

After just three days, Cheri and the kids fled in Davey's BMW, left without their clothes, and stayed with friends, sleeping on couches.

Cheri: I told Michelle we could buy new clothes, but she wanted me to go get her old clothes at the house. I took Ray and another friend back with me, and they stayed outside, with guns, and I got the clothes. All of a sudden, Davey was really nice, giving me a thousand dollars he had made hocking some [probably stolen] jewelry. He had never given me money.

Cheri took the kids to Magic Mountain for some fun before taking them home to Jerry in Fallon, Nevada. Davey went with them. On the drive, says Cheri, he acted completely normal, at least as "normal" as he had ever acted.

I was grateful that this was the case, since I wanted to be able to see my kids again.

After returning the kids to Jerry in Nevada, Cheri went back to Davey's place.

Judy: Okay, now I am screaming WHY, WHY, WHY?

Cheri: I remember thinking, I had lost everything already. But I had some personal things there. I had put a lot of work into fixing up this cabin. I thought, 'I'm not leaving with nothing again, I'm not doing it.' Also, he seemed to have softened as we drove the kids home.

Judy: The term "gaslighting" comes to mind.

Cheri: Once I returned, things got even worse. He actually nailed the windows shut so I couldn't get out. I would try to sleep, but he would turn up music full blast, on this huge stereo system he had, and start vacuuming. We had almost nothing in the house to eat. I was sleep deprived, isolated and hungry.

Davey had forced Cheri to give the motor home back to "Darryl," so she was totally dependent on Davey for transportation. She was a virtual prisoner, tortured by sleep deprivation from his loud music every night.

To this day, if I am forced to be locked into a room where someone is playing loud music, I find myself shaking uncontrollably.

The transcripts of Cheri's first parole board hearing, many years later, in Chino, California, indicate she suffered long-lasting trauma from this ordeal. She was questioned by her attorney about getting angry at another inmate for playing loud music, one of the very few psychological issues noted in her prison record.

Attorney: In your psychiatric eval, the evaluator comments back in 2005 when you had a mental health placement where there was a noise that made you sick...what was that about?

Inmate Mathews: I was having, I guess, PTSD issues with loud noises, loud music. David used to lock me in the house and turn the radio on full blast and keep me from sleeping. So now I have a thing where the loud music feels like abuse.

The abuse she suffered in 1998 would soon take more hideous forms.

Davey once woke me up in the middle of the night with a rifle at my head, talking to some "spirit" who was telling him to kill me. I got up naked and walked out of the front door and took off running. Ran naked into the desert. Davey got into his truck with off-road lights and chased me. I managed to stay out of the light beams by running and diving behind Joshua trees. Then I heard him calling, "Cheri, where are you? Please come home." When he caught up with me, he had no memory of what he did. Or at least, that's what he said.

Perhaps the worst abuse involved the way David Hepburn played on her protective feelings for the animals on their ranch. In addition to threatening to let them starve if she left him, Davey once pretended to have killed a bunch of newborn pups, sending her running towards the aqueduct where he claimed to have gutted them. After sobbing and searching, in vain, Cheri returned to the ranch to learn that he had hidden the puppies in boxes, retrieving them when she returned. Laughing. A total mind-fuck.

And then he kicked it up a notch. He told her he had buried her favorite puppy, Bosco. Buried him alive. And this time it wasn't a lie. More than a mind fuck, this was a soul-fuck.

I ran around looking for him, and saw the other pups digging near the porch. That was where Davey had buried him. I dug him out in time to rescue him.

Judy: And still, you stayed?

Cheri: If I hadn't been on meth, I would never have been there. Pure insanity. It was worse than I could ever describe. That I stayed in it was unimaginable.

She didn't stay much longer. But the details are buried forever in the haze of meth memory.

I left Davey for good some time in 1998. I don't remember the order of events. After I left him, with some jewelry and some clothes, I stayed with different friends, crashing on couches. I finally realized that he got off on torturing animals, on torturing me. I finally realized that I cannot save him and that he's insane. My daughter made me promise I would never go near him again.

If only.

Chapter 19

Getting Away with Murder, Redux

Back in 1995, you may recall, Cheri was interviewed by police about the death of Frank Belize while she was incarcerated in Nevada. She declined to tell them anything. Her children were also interviewed, but they had no relevant information. And since the body had never been found, it looked as though the case was going nowhere. It was, however, still an open case in 1998.

Cheri: After I left Davey, I was living with my friend, Joanne Courbot, and her son, Tim. Tim and I were cooking and dealing meth but we eventually had a falling out. Joanne remained my friend, and she was the one who told me that homicide detectives had called, looking for me. A drug task force had arrested Joey and they were planning to charge him with the murder of Frank Belize, because he had been overheard bragging about it. I also think they hoped he would give up information on drug deals.

Judy: But you still hadn't seen Joey since before you left for prison, right? And he did *not* kill Frank Belize.

Cheri: Right. Joey had joined the Mongols motorcycle gang and I got word that they were furious about Joey's arrest and were looking for me. They had gone to Davey's place, thinking they would find me there. They thought I was going to talk to the police and

confirm Joey's guilt. Davey told me the Mongols wanted to see me, that they had told him to call them if I should show up at his place.

Judy: So, let me get this straight. The police AND the Mongols are looking to talk to you?

Cheri: Yes. So I decided to face the Mongols, instead of waiting for them to find me. I called the vice president of the San Bernardino chapter of the Mongols and said, "Come get me and I'll talk to you." They sent a guy named Conan the Barbarian who brought me, on the back of his chopper, to the Vice President's house. Inside, they had set up this kind of "court" at a table with six of them sitting there, waiting to grill me.

Judy: That sounds fairly terrifying. I mean, the "San Bernardino Chapter of the Mongols" is hardly the Kiwanis Club.

Cheri: It was terrifying. My first words were, "Are you going to kill me?" And they said, "No, we just want to talk with you to get this story straight." Apparently Joey had bragged that he had killed Frank to protect me, and these guys thought I was responsible for Joey being in that situation.

Judy: So what did you tell them?

Cheri: The truth. I told them what actually happened that day: "I killed Frank Belize. Joey shot a dead body because he is a coward and a punk." And I told them I would turn myself in and get Joey out of jail. So the next day, I turned myself in to the cops, confessed, and Joey went free.

Judy: After what Joey had done to you, deserting you while you were in prison, that seems pretty big of you. Some might call it insane.

Cheri: I just felt I had to do the right thing. I lived by a certain code. Remember, right after it happened, I told everyone living in my house that I would take full responsibility, if it ever came to that. I even put on clean underwear because I thought I was going to go to jail. They interrogated me for at least four hours. Then they said I was free to go. "Just let us know where you are," they said.

Judy: That had to be shocking and freeing, at the same time.

Cheri: Shocking, but not totally freeing. Cops came to talk to me about the case again in 2010, when I was in prison. They have never closed the case, because even though I confessed, they had no evidence and could not charge me.

At Cheri's second parole hearing, many years later, a commissioner raised the issue of this open case regarding the demise of Frank Belize. These remarks are from the official transcript.

Deputy Commissioner Gardner: You know, there is no statute of limitations on murder. It's kind of a weird case. After doing thousands of (parole hearing) cases, I can't remember the last time where I was kind of thinking maybe somebody could be prosecuted [if released on parole]....It's kind of a weird case in that the government knows when you're testifying under oath that you say you shot and killed him. That's your testimony.

Inmate Mathews: Yes, I did, and I told them that in 1998. And I told them that again in 2010.

Deputy Commissioner Gardner: Does it bother you at all that... we could say, "Hey, let's let her go" and they might prosecute you? How do you feel about that?

Inmate Mathews: Well, I've expected it to happen over and over again. And it hasn't. So I'm not, I mean, I know the situation that happened with Frank. I know there were other people in the home when it happened. And in my mind, I was not going to get in that car with him. And I believed I was going to die. And I was very, very worried about that and what he would do to the rest of the house[hold] when it happened. So I know the truth. And if I go to court, then that's what's going to happen. And I'm okay with it. The thing is, I'm accountable. I'm accountable for that crime. I let that guy in my home. I endangered my children. I endangered my friends. And then I killed him. And that's my responsibility.

Cheri was released after her four-hour interrogation by police in 1998. She had dodged that bullet, to use an unfortunate metaphor, and returned immediately, full-time, to the manic meth cycle of cook-sell-use. It was so entwined with her everyday life, she packed the necessary cooking ingredients in a suitcase, for a trip to visit her daughter in Fallon, Nevada. She had to hitchhike, because she had no working vehicle at the time. But despite the obstacles, Cheri was determined to get there.

It was August, 1998. Michelle's birthday.

Chapter 20

Another Birthday, Another Bust

It is August 7th, and I'm in Carson City, Nevada, and it's 6 a.m. I am walking down highway 50. I have packed everything into a couple of suitcases, including my cooking stuff – a glass flask, some iodine and phosphorous. In fact, I have everything but the ephedrine, which I plan to get in Fallon. I get pulled over by the police for hitchhiking. Five cop cars and a K9 drug-sniffing unit. The cops want to search my luggage, but I say no. I have three grams of dope in my fanny pack and their special "dope sniffing" dog never reacts! A miracle. As there is no reason to get a search warrant, they are going to have to let me go. But one of the cops gets mad and when I start to leave, he is so angry, he throws me into the car and arrests me for the heck of it. They rip open my suitcase and find the lab stuff. They are really excited. One of them says, "You've got 25 years coming, bitch!"

But the joke was on them. I was charged but got out two weeks later, on my own recognizance. The charges were completely dismissed because they were based on an illegal search. The public defender tore them a new one.

Judy: But by then, you'd missed Michelle's birthday. Again.

Cheri: A lot of shit happened on their birthdays, with me trying to get to them. But I did manage to see them on the day I was released. I was wearing the only clothes I had left. All my stuff had

been taken when I was arrested, including Michelle's present. Michelle took me swimming in the irrigation ditch in Fallon, so my clothes were even worse after that. And then she told me it was Parents' Night at the school and she wanted me to meet her teachers.

Judy: So you went to her school with her? In the same clothes?

Cheri: Yes. Michelle introduced me to all her teachers. She didn't care what I looked like. But I was embarrassed. Because of the way I looked. Just because of who I was. Just out of jail, again. I remember thinking "I am such a loser." But Michelle didn't think so.

Cheri stayed for one day in Fallon, then headed back to her old stomping grounds in Phelan, in the California desert. She moved into a travel trailer in a junkyard owned by a man named Fred, a cross-dressing meth addict.

Cheri: Yep. "Cross-Dresser Fred." One of the local "characters." He asked me to keep an eye on the place. Gave me a gun. So I'm now living in a stolen trailer in a junkyard, pulling dirt out of the desert.

Judy: What do you mean, "pulling dirt out of the desert?"

Cheri: You could pull dope out of dirt, where Mexicans had been cooking in the desert. I found their dump site. I could dig and find the crystals from their cooking operation. I would dig up a bunch of it, put it in a kiddy pool, mix the dirt with water and lye. And use lighter fluid to pull the meth crystals out. I would cook it off with a little muriatic acid to get the PH to 7. Otherwise, you don't have any dope. It's a lot of work.

Judy: Sounds pretty desperate.

Cheri. Yeah. But I was a cook and knew what I was doing. And by now, I am also sick in the head, using meth. I was fucking done. This was a bottom. But not really. I had further down to go.

Pulling dope out of dirt in the desert, cooking it up in a kiddy pool, living in a junkyard – these definitely are mile markers on the road to desperation and demoralization. And then, just when she was at her lowest, Cheri got a message that an officer with a drug task force wanted to talk with her on the phone.

The guy's name was Ray Carusco. I later learned that he was with the San Bernardino sheriff's office, part of a tri-county drug task force. He tells me he knows what Davey has done to me and wants me to help bust him. I told him no way. I told Joanne that I needed to go out to Davey's and warn him. She told me to forget him, don't go out there.

But I have to go.

Cheri went to Davey's ranch, the place they had shared before she finally managed to leave six months before, leaving behind most of her belongings. She went to warn him that the police were after him. But when she got there, he refused to open the door.

He turns the music on full blast inside the house. I had hitchhiked and walked there from Phelan to warn him and I'm hurt. So I wrote him a long note, a letter, telling him about the cops asking me to alert them when the Mexicans were there, cooking on his property. I wanted to warn him. I don't remember the whole note, but I left it on his door.

From the transcript of her second parole hearing, April, 2014:

INMATE MATHEWS: I wrote him a letter that was personal. I was trying to warn him that the police had been contacting me. He made copies of the letter and started passing it around. A friend came to the property that I was staying on and told me there's a letter being passed around town and David had said that I was trying to set up him and the Mexicans and that they were going to kill me for it.

And so, I got upset. Very upset. And I called the police back and told them I would help them. And I told Mr. Carusco at that time that I had already been out to warn David and that now I was pissed off and I wanted to help them.

If Davey was going to put a snitch jacket on me, I might as well be a snitch.

From the transcript of the first parole board hearing:

INMATE MATHEWS: I was humiliated. It was bad enough that he had abused me and that I had left with nothing. And now he had betrayed me, putting a snitch jacket on me.

And so, I wanted revenge. I wanted to put him in jail. I wanted him to know how it felt. I wanted to take everything he owned. And I wanted him to suffer the way that I believed he had made me suffer.

PRESIDING COMMISSIONER ROBERTS: How much do you think the methamphetamine had to do it?

INMATE MATHEWS: It had just about everything to do with it, the meth. It had never before occurred to me to go get revenge on anybody for anything. That changed in that last eight years of my meth addiction, my whole personality changed. I just really changed into a different person.

Chapter 21

The Murder Of David Hepburn

And so, we arrive at that place where every pogonip of rage, low self-esteem, abuse, addiction, self-sabotage and a seething resentment against bullies converge to create the toxic conditions for murder.

Cheri: Davey was telling people I was setting him up, as well as the Mexicans. That scared me. They would kill me. I hid my fear with anger. I was a walking time bomb. They called me Scary Cheri. I was sick to death of trying to be loyal to men who would rather see me dead.

From the parole board transcript, April 2014:

INMATE MATHEWS: He had hurt me, abused me, used me, thrown me away because he could. And that was who he was. And he did it because he just thought he could get away with it. And I was not going to let him get away with it. It was just like all the men in my life I've let hurt me. And that was my belief back then, that I was the victim.

But while revenge was on her mind, murder was not. Premeditation requires a homicidal pathology, not to mention a clear mind. Cheri had neither.

Out of defiance and a desire for revenge I called Ray Carusco and told him I would help them get Davey. He picked me up at my friend

Bambi's house and we drove out to the hills above Davey's ranch with binoculars. He said he needed me because I could get near Davey. He asked me how I would get on the ranch and I told him that Davey still had everything I owned and I would go over there and ask for my things back.

Carusco told me they would give me witness protection, money, whatever I wanted. I told him I would only help him get Davey, not the Mexicans. They hadn't done anything to me and I wanted no beef with them. What I was supposed to do was find out when the meth was being cooked on the property and give him a call.

As soon as I cooled down, I began to regret what I had done.

Judy: I wondered when the "code" would kick in.

Cheri: All I had to do was call them when the cooking was going on and the police would raid the place. They were going to let me have my things back. They were going to pay me and I was going to leave town and start my life again. But I couldn't do it. All that went right out the window because of the guilt I felt for going against the code.

Cheri had written extensively in her prison bio about the family "code" and the rule against snitching. The parole board members who questioned her in 2014 had read her bio and were very interested in how those early lessons had impacted her behavior leading up to the murder.

INMATE MATHEWS: My father was very much against the establishment. So I was raised with a belief system that the police were the bad guys. There was a lot of prejudice in my family.

DEPUTY COMMISSIONER MARTIN: Against the police?

INMATE MATHEWS: Against police, against other cultures and even against people with money. My dad was just very angry at his station in life, I believe. And so he put a lot of that on me. We had that certain belief system we were raised with.

DEPUTY COMMISSIONER MARTIN: One way I saw you programmed to have criminalistic thinking was how you reacted to being called a snitch.

INMATE MATHEWS: Yeah. That was a huge deal.

DEPUTY COMMISSIONER MARTIN: I think that would have rolled off a lot of people. It really made you angry.

INMATE MATHEWS: I think a lot of that had to do with my mother when I was young. That really made an impact on me, her calling me a snitch and then leaving me, leaving my life for those years. It made an impact.

Cheri was torn between keeping her promise to Carusco, thus adhering to that part of the "Code" that honors keeping one's word, and adhering to the part that forbids "snitching." The meth that had set up permanent residence in her brain was certainly not helping with her critical thinking skills. Deeply depressed, Cheri once again thought suicide might be a reasonable option.

I was sick of myself and my life. I had a .22 caliber pistol in my trailer that Fred, the junkyard owner, had given to me for protection. I took the gun and drove my truck out to the desert near Davey's place. I put the gun in my mouth.

Then I thought of my kids. Thought of all the hurt Davey had caused me and the women before me. I had made a deal with Carusco and I had to be brave enough to see it through. I realized suicide was the cowardly way out.

From the transcripts of her second parole hearing in 2014:

PRESIDING COMMISSIONER ROBERTS: Why did you go over to his [David's] house?

INMATE MATHEWS: Originally, my intent was to do what the police asked me and set him up. That was what I wanted to do. That was my intent of how I was going to get my things back and get some money and get out of town. The minute I pulled up to the house and I saw the motorhome backed up to the barn, and I thought the Mexicans were there, I just forgot about all that. I grabbed the gun. And I was going to go out shooting. I was suicidal. And I believe I was already looking for a reason to shoot him. And he gave me the reason.

COMMISSIONER ROBERTS: So you think you went there, went into the house with the intent to kill him?

INMATE MATHEWS: Yes, I do. I don't think I wanted to admit that, but yes.

COMMISSIONER ROBERTS: When did you get that formulation? When did it change from going over to set him up for the police?

INMATE MATHEWS: Right when I pulled up. Right when I pulled up, I saw the motorhome. The motorhome backed up to the barn. And I thought the Mexicans are really here, this is really happening. What I was supposed to be there for the police was to see if there was cooking going on at the property, then to call them and let them know. If I had been wanting to continue with the police deal, I would have just driven away right then and got on the phone. And so obviously that was when it just changed for me. I wasn't going to go through with the police thing. Screw it. I'm going to go out shooting.

The generator in the motor home was running and I was convinced the Mexicans were in the barn cooking. They were really there and they would kill me. I pulled the gun out from under the seat of the truck. I was high and I felt myself becoming detached by the fear I felt. I knocked on the door.

Davey answered. "What in the hell do you want?" Then he went inside and sat down on the couch. It was L-shaped with a very large slice of a tree trunk for a coffee table. He was sitting and I was standing. "Why would you put a snitch jacket on me and put me in danger?" I asked. "I came here and warned you and you lied. Why would you do that to me?"

Davey said, "Because I can. You are dead, bitch, and you don't even know it." I said I wanted my things back. He said "You're not getting them. And I know where your friends are, I know where your kids live."

I said, "I want my shit and I want to get out of here." Then I started walking toward a lamp that belonged to me and he jumped off the couch.

INMATE MATHEWS: That's when I pulled a gun. In hindsight, I think he just was going to stop me from trying to grab the lamp.

COMMISSIONER FERGUSON: So why did you shoot him?

INMATE MATHEWS: Once I pulled the gun, I just started shooting. Rage. I'd have to say rage. Rage that I believed that he thought he could do anything he wanted and get away with it. And I had a gun that day.

I don't even remember pulling out the gun. I emptied it and I was screaming. He stumbled back around the coffee table and lay bent over the couch breathing hard. I was still screaming. I don't know how long I screamed. When I stopped, it was so quiet.

I knew the Mexicans were going to shoot me as soon as I ran out the door. I started to re-load the gun and was sure Davey would jump up at any minute. There was no blood that I could see and no bullet wounds, so I thought he was faking it and I was sure Davey was going to jump up. Davey had played so many sick games on me, I was sure he wasn't really dead.

Judy: In every account of this, whether it's to the parole board, in your bio, in our conversations, you seem to remember the smallest details.

Cheri: Fear causes me to become detached. The whole conversation is vivid.

Judy: But fear also led you to believe that the Mexicans were there, and would kill you. And yet, you later found out that the Mexicans were never there. The motorhome was occupied by a woman who was staying there.

Cheri: Her name was Jan. She was the one who found Davey's body the next day and called the police. But that night, I drove like a maniac to get away. I kept looking in the rear view mirror to see if the Mexicans were chasing me. When I realized I wasn't being chased, I stopped the truck and buried the gun in the desert.

Judy: But that wasn't the end of it, right?

Cheri: No. I got my friends Bonnie and Kenny to take me back out to Davey's ranch to see if he was really dead.

Judy: Those are some friends.

Cheri: Bonnie didn't want to go inside, but Kenny did. He came out to the truck, pretty shaken, and said, Yes, Davey is really dead. Then I went inside and got my jewelry box and clothes and left. If he [Davey] had just talked to me, apologized for putting a snitch jacket on me, if I hadn't had a gun that night, it would have turned out different.

Judy: So how long did it take before the cops came to get you?

Cheri: I killed him on the day before Thanksgiving, just before my birthday. I was arrested two weeks later. I was cooking dope upstairs at a friend's house, and I heard them come through the front door. I didn't want my friend in trouble - she had no idea about the murder- so I ran downstairs and gave myself up. I confessed later that night. I just broke down. I was ready. My life was over and I knew it. I was actually relieved.

Judy: Did you ever hear from the cop who enlisted you as an informant?

Cheri: Carusco never showed up or backed me up. He didn't give a shit. That's the way cops work. I was nothing to them. Just a dope fiend. The police report didn't mention it.

From the official police report:

"Defendant used a .22 caliber handgun to shoot victim three times in the torso, causing the victim's death. Victim was the defendant's former boyfriend, and they resided together off and on for one to two years. Defendant indicated that victim was very jealous and played cruel mind games with her. Defendant indicated that the victim cooked methamphetamine on his property with the Mexican Mafia. According to defendant, victim threatened to have the Mexican Mafia kill her and she became angry. She took a .22 caliber pistol out of her pocket and shot the victim while he was seated on the living room couch."

From parole board transcripts:

COMMISSIONER FERGUSON: What were you upset with David about?

INMATE MATHEWS: Betrayal, betraying me, putting a snitch jacket on me, spreading the letter I wrote to him around town. I was humiliated. It was bad enough that he had abused me and that I left with nothing, and even then – tried to be loyal to him. So I wanted revenge. I wanted to take everything he owned. And I wanted him to suffer the way that I believed he had made me suffer. Because I was totally in a victim role. I thought I was the victim. He was the villain.

Cheri was arrested on December 2nd, 1998.

She was 38 years old. Her daughter Michelle was 13, Jason 10. "When I heard she was arrested for murder," Michelle told me, "I was relieved. I was glad she was finally safe. And ALIVE. I mean, she was still my Mom."

Chapter 22

Send Me an Angel Named Yolanda

From the Antelope Valley edition of the *Daily News*, December 4, 1998:

Woman to be arraigned in Llano shooting death: Former boyfriend's past mistreatment, keeping of her belongings cited as motives

"Cheri Mathews of Phelan is expected to be arraigned today on murder charges in the death of David Hepburn, who was found shot to death November 19 at his isolated ranch.

'She was upset that he wouldn't return her personal items and about his past mental games,' Los Angeles County Sheriff's Department Homicide Detective Ignacio Reyes said Thursday. 'It all culminated in her mind, and she killed him. At times, he wouldn't treat her nicely or give her the respect that she thought she deserved.'

'Information on the street was that she had committed the murder,' said Reyes. 'She came into the station for us to interview her. Her story didn't match. She had more information than us. Eventually she confessed.'"

The newspaper article was factual. So was the police report. But reading them now, with all I know about Cheri's life, from the cruelty of her childhood to the addictive insanity of adulthood, with her late father's voice playing, relentlessly, in her head, I realized how shallow those reports were. Her "former boyfriend's past mistreatment?" Gaslighting, mind-fucking, and psychological torture by a dangerous psychopath is surely a more accurate description. And that line about being "upset because he wouldn't return her personal items?" That sounds like the most shallow motive imaginable. I kept thinking of Cheri's repeated references, during our conversations and in her prison autobiography, to the importance of holding on to the few belongings she had, as evidence that, dammit, she was a person to be reckoned with, a person who had lost so much, and couldn't bear to lose any more. Her "personal items" symbolized her sense of self-worth, her very soul. And yet, facts are facts and murder is murder and Cheri would have the rest of her life to come to terms with those facts.

From Cheri's prison autobiography:

I struggle with a lot of demons, mostly the memories of my insanity, the shame of who I was and what I did, the guilt and remorse of not being a good enough mother, and remorse over my choices. The other struggle is that although I am sorry for what I did, I am not sorry my victims are dead. I try to imagine them making different choices, changing their lives as I did. Did I rob them of that opportunity? I will never know. I only know what they had done in the past they had every intention of continuing and if I saved one person from them I cannot be sorry.

Following her arrest for the murder of David Hepburn in 1998, Cheri was immediately transferred to the Twin Towers Correctional Facility in downtown Los Angeles. Although the jail had been opened just the year before, it would eventually be singled out as one of the ten worst prisons in the United States, according to reporting by *Mother Jones* magazine, because of overcrowding and assaults by guards. Now and then, a celebrity inmate would do a brief stint there. Paris Hilton, for one, who was housed in the medical unit, apart from other inmates, at a cost to taxpayers of more than a thousand dollars a day.

That was not Cheri's experience. Her experience of the place was traumatic and dramatic.

Cheri: L.A. County Jail is a nut ward. When you arrive, they put you in a long hallway where you stand in a long line of 30 girls. You have to strip. If you have a tampon, you have to pull it out right there. Turn around, hands on the wall, cough while they shine a flashlight up your butt. They put me in the mental pod for three days. I could not stop crying. I was coming off drugs, detoxing without meds. My brain had stopped producing its own serotonin, because meth had done that job for so long. And I was sleepy and depressed. Totally defeated.

Judy: Why were you placed in the mental unit?

Cheri: I was on suicide watch. But I knew that once I got transferred to the regular pod, I could get a razor like all the other inmates. I was planning to end my life once I got that razor. That's all I could think about.

Judy: What changed your mind?

Cheri: An inmate named Yolanda. A Black prostitute. She had a room in the mental pod, with a bunk. I was on suicide watch, sleeping on the floor on a mat. She put her hand on my shoulder and said, "God wants me to talk with you right now." And she

offered to share her room. "God has a plan for you," she said. "Jesus loves you and he forgives you."

Judy: I have to say, if a person in a mental unit of a prison started talking about God to me and offered to share her room, I would not be inclined to listen.

Cheri: Are you kidding? I was *aching* for redemption. The alternative was suicide. She was the first person to offer hope. I will never forget her. I admit that when she first said those words, I said, "Lady, you don't know me and Jesus does not love me." But she would not give up. She said, "I wouldn't waste my time if He hadn't talked to me about you." When we got out of the mental pod, I went to a church service in the prison. They said, "Anyone who wants to accept Jesus Christ in their heart, stand up." I did. I was crying. I thought I had surrendered and that I had a clean slate. I felt very light, even happy. But I also thought my decision meant I could never sin again. I had never been to church before. I knew nothing. My dad was the only God I had known. So I figured the conditions were simple: You accept Jesus as your savior, you can't make another mistake. I didn't know.

Judy: What happened when you were put back in the regular pod?

Cheri: I got into it with another inmate, almost right away. I was on sweeping duty, sweeping the floor in the pod. But I swept too close to this one woman's feet, and she yelled at me. Jesus hadn't given me any social skills yet, so I hit her. She was very big. She picked me up and threw me against the wall and I started to pound her face. The guards tore my rotator cuff getting me off her. She tore my face with her nails. Now my arm was in a sling and I was put in "the hole."

Judy: How did that affect your new-found faith?

Cheri: In my mind, I had violated the conditions of being saved. I thought once you had been saved, you couldn't sin again. So I thought it was null and void. But in solitary, I was given a blanket and a Bible to read. And I had visions of what my life in prison was going to be. Fighting, drugging, drinking. I had already been there, done that. I had never seen consequences before. That's when I got on my knees. I made a decision, at long last, to surrender. This wasn't someone else's idea of faith. This was my own prayer, born out of total desperation. "God, I don't know who you are, but I need help. If you're real, help me. Help me change. I don't want to be this person." And I made that decision, in the hole, on my knees, to give up my ego, to give up choosing violence and drugs over everything else.

Judy: A surrender.

Cheri: A surrender. At last.

Chapter 23

To Plead or Not to Plead:
Is There a Question?

Cheri was in Twin Towers for about three weeks, but that was enough time to contemplate suicide, get rescued by one inmate and get into a brawl with another, get a torn rotator cuff, serve some time in "the hole," hit bottom at long last, pray for help from a higher power, and go to court for her sentencing. She also found time to do some rescuing of her own.

Palma Kuykendall Paxton arrived at Twin Towers just a few days before Cheri was brought in. Palma told me Cheri saved her from a beating by a bully. Familiar turf for Cheri. But not for Palma, who had been convicted of defrauding her employer, a well-known Hollywood producer.

"I was sentenced in 1998 for credit card fraud. Six months at County. I was a low-level offender and should never have been sentenced there. It was a scary place. Whites and Blacks kept to themselves. There was very little mixing. I don't know why this one Black woman had it in for me, but she started coming at me, to hit me, to hurt me. Cheri, this 6-foot tall, strong woman with long, red hair, stepped right in front of me, to protect me. The woman backed down, immediately. Cheri was that imposing. She didn't even have to put her fists up."

"I was so grateful to her for standing up for me at a time when no else did. She was transferred to a state prison in Chowchilla, so I had lost my protector. But she wrote me a letter when she left. I saved it."

Dear Palma,

Thank you for being my friend. You helped me so much. You are a Godsend. Remember your priorities when you leave here. I hope I hear from you and it's all good news, but I'll hear the bad, too. Never, ever forget how beautiful you are, inside and out.

Love,

Cheri Lee Mathews

Palma says her nose was broken by another inmate the night before she was released. "Cheri was no longer there to protect me."

"My father," she adds, "told me to never look back, never be in touch with anyone there. That life was gone and I was trying to re-invent myself. So I never told anybody that I kept in touch with Cheri. It took me 7 years, until 2005, to find her and start writing her in prison. I had her name and did some research. We started writing back and forth. She would send me a list of things she needed and I would send her a money order. I eventually got to visit her in Valley State Prison for Women. She seemed smaller than I remembered. In my mind, she was my big protector. Bigger than life. She was selfless. And fearless. She was a force to be reckoned with."

Many years later, when Cheri was finally eligible for a hearing before the parole board, one of the many letters written to the board came from Palma Kuykendall Paxton.

While all this personal drama was unfolding at L.A. County Jail, the legal drama was taking place at the county courthouse in Lancaster, where Cheri first met her court-appointed lawyer, Manuel

Martinez, the day after her arrest. Martinez managed to work out a plea deal for Cheri.

Cheri: I had already confessed to killing Davey so I knew there was no defense. I remember just giving up. A hopelessness. I cried in court, cried in the holding cell. Just curled up in a ball and slept. Nobody wanted to hear my side of things, how I had made a deal with a cop to see if Davey was cooking. But, of course, nobody told me to take a gun with me, flip out and kill him. So there was no defense.

According to the official court transcripts, the judge made Cheri's options very clear.

Q. Miss Mathews, you are charged in this felony complaint with unlawfully and with malice aforethought murdering one David Hepburn. Do you understand that charge, Ma'am?

A. Yes, sir.

Q. The maximum punishment as I've calculated it along with your attorney is if the jury was to find you guilty of this offense in the first degree, the sentence would be a required sentence of 25 years to life. Additionally the use of a firearm is...by itself 25 years to life for a total of 50 years to life if you were to be convicted of the maximum punishment.

Now, even if you were convicted of second degree murder, which is 15 to life, you would still have the gun enhancement use of a firearm allegation which would add 25 years to the 15 years which would still give you 40 years to life and your attorney indicated to me you wish to take simply the 15 years to life without the gun enhancement and then, hopefully, apply for release and parole at the time you're eligible for parole release. Do you understand that?

Yes, sir.

Q. Is that what you wish to do?

A. Yes, sir.

Given the options, the second degree murder charge with no gun enhancement, resulting in 15 to life with the possibility of parole at 15 years, sounds like a very good deal. In fact, the County Prosecutor and Chief Probation Officer had asked for a tougher sentence, with no parole. In their official filing, they quoted Homicide Detective Ignacio Reyes as pointing out that "defendant is the primary suspect in another murder case. Reyes stated that defendant murdered another boyfriend a few years ago in San Bernardino County and they have been unable to locate the body. He stated that charges have not been filed because they have been unable to locate enough evidence. Officer Reyes indicated that defendant confessed to the murder but claimed self-defense. The victim was shot in the head. Officer Reyes indicated his belief that the defendant deserves more time in prison than the 15 years to life plea agreement."

The prosecutor's statement also brought up Cheri's "serious substance abuse problem. Defendant's personal use and involvement with methamphetamine no doubt contributed to her violent behavior resulting in the shooting death of the victim. A substantial state prison sentence is warranted."

Cheri was not privy to these statements when her lawyer convinced her to take the plea deal. But she would learn about them after having second thoughts on accepting that deal. Why the second thoughts? From prison, she called her trusted friend Al, who had once allowed her to stay at his place when she ran away from Davey. And Al advised her not to take the plea deal.

Cheri: He said, 'That's not a deal, a life sentence is not a deal! Grey Davis is governor and his motto is *a life for a life*. He never

grants parole to lifers!' That freaked me out and I tried to withdraw my plea.

Cheri's attorney, Manny Martinez, got her a hearing before another judge and tried to explain Cheri's reasoning for retracting her plea.

Mr. Martinez: Your honor....at the time of taking of the plea, she says she was coming down from the effects of drug usage and that she didn't fully appreciate what she was doing at the time.

The Defendant: It happened so fast. Just, I was under a lot of duress. It was the day after I had been arrested, the plea bargain, and I just want a chance to tell my side of it.

And so, Cheri was assigned a second public defender to help her consider whether to withdraw her initial plea.

Cheri: It didn't take long for me to change my mind again. The new lawyer, I can't remember his name now, just that he wore cowboy boots, thought he was real slick, and that he had seen the filing about the earlier murder. Frank Belize. "I'll tell you what you're looking at. Take this plea or else they will charge you with the other murder and you are never going to get out." I was crying. This was my lawyer telling me this. He was not at all sympathetic. So I retracted my retraction.

Her original public defender, Manny Martinez, was still by her side when Cheri went to court for sentencing two days after Christmas, 1998. She was given 15 to life for second degree murder.

Cheri: I was crying at sentencing. It was an out-of-body experience. I had no family there. They had had it with me. I chose drugs, murder, over my children. But a realization had come to me even before I was sentenced. I was a coward, even though I had spent

my whole life trying to be brave. **Killing Davey was a way out of my life. I had gone to the desert to kill myself but I killed him instead. What a selfish way to save my life.**

Judy: Your crime saved your life?

Cheri: Prison saved my life.

But it would take years before Cheri would be deeply grateful for this chance to construct a new life. To reach the point where she could say, "Prison saved my life." That December day in 1998, listening to her sentence read in court, crying and alone, Cheri was at the bottom of all those bottoms that came before. And yet, she still managed to touch other people. She had touched Palma, certainly, who would never forget her. But also Manny Martinez, her court-appointed lawyer. In handwritten notes from her case file, Martinez wrote the following on the day of sentencing:

"She thanked me for all I did for her. Also apologized for all the trouble she had been. Was led away with a tear in her eye and a smile on her face."

Chapter 24

Mitigating Factors

When Cheri received her 15 to life sentence in the Los Angeles County Court, she did not believe she would ever be paroled. Lifers were in for life, she figured, especially under the policies of then-Governor Grey Davis. Her friend Al had been quite accurate about his information: Davis, a Democrat, was trying to prove he was tougher on crime than his Republican opponent. In fact, in 1998, Davis was establishing himself as more conservative on criminal justice issues than almost any other elected official in the nation. He essentially removed the "time off for good behavior" incentive by refusing any recommendation the parole board made to grant a release. He announced that any judge he appointed should reflect those harsh policies "or resign."

Reading the report written by the chief probation officer of L.A. County, submitted to the sentencing judge in Cheri's case, it is clear that her sentence could have been much more severe, with no possibility of parole at all. It is a cold, hard look at her crime, outlining "aggravating factors" and "mitigating factors."

AGGRAVATING FACTORS:

1. **The crime involved great violence, great bodily harm, threat of great bodily harm, or other acts disclosing a high degree of cruelty, viciousness, or callousness.**

2. **The defendant was armed with or used a weapon at the time of the commission of the crime.**
3. **The planning, sophistication or professionalism with which the crime was carried out, or other facts, indicated premeditation.**
4. **The defendant has engaged in a pattern of violent conduct which indicates a serious danger to society.**
5. **The defendant's prior convictions as an adult or adjudications of commission of crimes as a juvenile are numerous or of increasing seriousness.**
6. **The defendant has served prior prison terms.**
7. **The defendant's prior performance on probation or parole was unsatisfactory.**

MITIGATING FACTORS:
NONE

None? NONE? Cheri's whole life up to that point was a mitigating factor, starting with the emotional and physical trauma of her home life, sexual abuse by the neighbors, the abandonment and rejection of her mother, the school years of repeated suspensions when no one thought to recommend counseling or medication, to near-death experiences with crashing planes, a knife-wielding rapist, and a couple of sociopaths who tortured her emotionally and threatened her friends and family. Also, the meth. Always, the meth.

Clearly, I was not an objective reader of this report. But then, I had the benefit of the bigger picture, one that did not include words like "cruelty, viciousness, callousness" or "sophisticated ... premeditation."

Sophisticated premeditation? Cheri's state of mind the night she drove into the desert with a gun, suicide on her mind, a mind racing on meth, abruptly changing course to Davey's place to confront him about his betrayal, *that* state of mind was neither "sophisticated" nor "premeditated."

But it was murder. Mitigating factors -even if they had been considered – could not change that fact. Even so, Cheri would have years to contemplate her own motives that night, to understand all the triggers that prompted her to actually pull the trigger. And for a long time, she convinced herself that her fears for her children's safety played a part.

Cheri: I had so much guilt about my kids. And Davey knew where my kids lived. My guilt, my fear for them, went into rage. And my rage said, 'I have to take you out.'

Judy: As you heard the sentence, 15 to life, were your kids on your mind then, too?

Cheri: I was going to prison. I thought I would never get out. My remorse was so deep, it was the darkest place I had ever been. Knowing I would not be with my kids, I was so ashamed, so embarrassed. I couldn't even make the phone call to tell them what happened. I did call Jerry, and he told me Michelle was relieved, because she thought I would at least be safe. I thought they were better off without me. I was so screwed up. I hated myself with every fiber of my being.

Judy: What happened after sentencing?

Cheri: I was sent to the women's prison in Chowchilla. County was awful, so I felt I was lucky to be transferred quickly and get out of there. Chowchilla and Valley State Prison for Women [VSPW] are very rough prisons, not far from each other.

Judy: How was the trip up there?

Cheri: We were all shackled on the bus. And it was a long way. I was miserable. I talked to other women prisoners on the way up. We were all talking shit to hide our fear. The windows on prison buses are covered with mesh, so the world you are leaving is already fading away.

Judy: I've always wondered what's going through the minds of inmates on those prison buses.

Cheri: Throughout your prison time, you get shipped to places, like going to court or to the dentist. You are shackled on a bus, mesh on the windows. Sometimes murderers are put in cages on the bus, with armed guards watching us. You're looking at life happening outside this box. The despair is so deep. Life is right outside this window. People are walking their dogs, going shopping. I realize I can't reach it. And I may never reach it again. Then, when I would get to the dentist's office, I was led through the waiting room in shackles and handcuffs. Sitting in the dentist's chair, looking out the window, thinking, "it's just there. So close, the real world." Every bus trip was agonizing.

Judy: What happened when you arrived in Chowchilla?

Cheri: When we got to Chowchilla, the intake was not too bad. Better than LA County. We were strip searched, then led into receiving. Four or five concrete cells, concrete benches inside the cells. They put us in muumuus, handed us a set of red prison clothes. Then we were packed into the cells with everyone who just got off the bus.

Judy: After that?

Cheri: They did all our paperwork, gave us our bedding, then assigned each of us to a bunk in a big building with tiers of cells.

Cheri had made some friends in her short stay in the Intake section of Chowchilla, and was hoping that's where she would serve her time. But her file identified her as "gang-affiliated," because of the Mexican cartel connection, and prisoners with gang connections were transferred to Valley State Prison for Women. And so, after 6 weeks in Chowchilla, she was moved again.

Cheri: I got scared. I didn't know anyone at VSP. I had no chance to acclimate. I had heard horrid things about it. So, another bus, another shackling, another intake process. We got blue outfits, muumuus and bedding. I was put in an eight-women cell.

Her new address:
Cheri Mathews #78136 B2-12-1UP
Valley State Prison for Women
Chowchilla, Ca. 93610-0092

It was 1999. She would remain there until 2011, when the facility was turned into a men's prison and she would be transferred yet again. But for 12 years, VSPW would be home.

Chapter 25

Life in a Gated Community

Valley State Prison for Women in Chowchilla, California, was essentially a gated community from hell, one with few amenities and even fewer trustworthy residents. Cheri took advantage, from the get-go, of everything the prison did offer, from church to the gym and track to classes to AA and NA meetings. In other words, she approached this challenge with the same full-out energy, bordering on mania, that had informed every other part of her life.

Cheri: I wasn't looking for a reward. I just wanted desperately to change. I wanted to have integrity in my life, sort of the reverse side of that old criminal code integrity. I wanted to stop doing anything wrong. And I *was* trustworthy. Others were not. If they could get away with something, they would. They would be one person in program, another person in the cell. They were not trying to change. They were trying to "get over." My challenge in prison was to choose integrity even when no one was looking. I had to speak the truth, if I wanted to keep a conscious contact with God. At the same time, it was hard keeping myself in check, not to take on that prison mentality. You have people who run things and they make it hard on the newcomers. Treat you like you're a piece of shit. Some

girls were so bad they wouldn't let you use the bathroom in the cell. Women can be fucking horrible, Judy.

Judy: Tell me about the cell.

Cheri: They put me on B yard, general population. 8 women to a cell. The cell had concrete floors, two sinks, one shower, one toilet with a door. But the door had big holes in it so the guards could shine a light and see you. Four bunk beds, a back window on the yard, front window on the hallway. Each inmate had a locker. When I first came in, only one girl was there. She was asleep in the middle of the day, with a beanie over her eyes. I came in with all my stuff, bedding and all this crap. I'd been up since 4 a.m., going through intake, trying to be quiet. She made some smart ass remark like "get in here and do what you have to do." So I did. Made my bed on the top middle bunk, the worst one, with no privacy, put my stuff in my locker. I didn't say shit. Other girls came in and were friendly. I noticed they avoided the other girl.

Judy: So it went all right then?

Cheri: No. I started to get dressed and that girl – her name is Sylvia Arizmendi – went nuts. "Go change in the bathroom!! NOT in this room!" I had never shared a room with so many people. I said, "If that's the rule, not a problem." But *she* was a problem. She was a fucking bully, big and mean.

Judy: What was she in prison for?

Cheri: She was doing life without [parole]. For robbing and tying up an old lady. She terrorized her. The old woman died of a stroke during the robbery.

Judy: Was she your bunkmate?

Cheri: No, my first Bunkie was Carmen Garcia. She did tattoos for inmates in exchange for drugs. We got along fine. I actually got along with everyone. I tried to share the gifts I got in the mail, tried to be friendly. That made Sylvia jealous. We ended up getting into it.

Judy: What happened?

Cheri: She was bullying another woman, and I jumped down and told her, "Let's do it." But she wouldn't get off her bunk and engage with me. So I asked for a bed move, and then everyone else in the cell did the same. They were scared to stay without me there to protect them. So we all moved to different rooms. For a while, she was left alone in there. I actually felt bad. But we never talked again.

Judy: Why did you challenge her? Weren't you trying to avoid confrontation and fighting?

Cheri: Yes. But I was never the aggressor. I would only flip out in defense of others. Then I would lose control. I never got caught, never got punished for it. The guards would look the other way if I was scaring off bullies. I remember one guard said, "Wipe the blood off your face, Cheri," and then he walked on by.

Cheri was a good judge of character, which would serve her well during her years of incarceration. Her assessment of Sylvia Arizmendi was spot on. I came across this 1996 article in the *L.A. Times*, with an award-worthy lede:

Death by Fright at Issue in Murder Trial

Sylvia Arizmendi stands accused of scaring someone to death. The victim, Bertha Kavanaugh, was an 86-year-old woman with slightly hardened arteries and a satchel full of $20 bills.

Judy: You mentioned that your first bunkmate, Carmen, gave women tattoos in exchange for drugs. How did the drugs get inside the prison?

Cheri: Some of the inmates worked outside as farm workers and they would act as mules, bringing the drugs in. If they didn't get the stuff, they would be beaten, even raped. One inmate got her drugs in packages sent to her through the prison chaplain, a little old lady who never suspected she was being used.

Judy: And you were never tempted to use again?

Cheri: I was offered crack cocaine once. I ran the whole tape in my head. What it would taste like, how it would feel, how I'd get more, the whole sick deal. And then I said no. It was the first time I had ever turned down drugs in my entire life.

Judy: And that was it?

Cheri: That was it. I came close once when I was working in the automotive unit. A girl named Shorty had laid out lines of meth on my desk. My body started to react before my brain could kick in, and I actually started to bend over and do it. Then I stopped myself and told her to get it off my desk.

Cheri had always been manic when it came to cleaning, even when she was immersed in the meth life. That talent would prove invaluable in prison, where eight women sharing a cell and one bathroom could lead to serious trouble.

Cheri: People got so crazy. If there was a hair in the shower, bullies would shame people, scream "You dirty bitch!" I tried to talk to women about it. "Be sure to wash out the sink after you brush your teeth, flush more than once after you poop so it doesn't stink up the room," things like that. I had the training from home and from the Army, so I was a very good roommate. But I hated snorers.

Judy: Oh my God, that would be horrible.

Cheri: Yeah. Snorers would get abused. I would try to roll them over, but even with earbuds in, and the fan on, you could hear them. If a snorer was in the bunk below me, I would tie a string to her toe and then yank it whenever she started to snore. It worked.

Judy: Sounds like you had to be fairly inventive.

Cheri: In all sorts of ways. I made a great cheese cake in prison, out of sprite, lemon juice, dry dairy creamer, graham crackers and butter.

Just a few months after Cheri arrived at VSPW in 1999, she met another newcomer, Claudia Chita.

"I was serving 7 years for assault and battery," she told me in a phone interview, "so I was a long-termer and she was a lifer. I left in 2006, and we were friends the whole time, two years in the same cell. She was my bunkie. When I first met Cheri, I had been in a fight with someone in my cell, and I had a black eye. So they moved me to Cheri's cell. She said she would protect me. And pretty soon, she got her chance."

A woman named India was among those sharing that cell. Claudia says she was a violent psychopath.

"An absolute lunatic. One day she'd say she was Muslim, another day Native American. She took everything to weird, twisted levels. She was a raging rhinoceros. I'll never forget when she went after me. Cheri jumped down from her bunk, took India by the throat and pushed her up against the wall. Not to injure her, but to stop the situation. India left me alone after that."

"We used to walk the track every day, as long as we could," Claudia added. "We talked about our lives and our dreams. We talked about what we heard on the TV news, and tried to make sense of it. When everyone was talking about Y2K and what it might mean, we had a plan.

We wondered if the water would stop running, so we stored bags of water in the shower."

[Y2K refers to potential computer errors related to the formatting for dates after the year 2000. Computer systems' inability to distinguish dates correctly had the potential for creating chaos for industry, air travel, and banking. By the time the turn of the century arrived, pre-emptive action had been taken and nothing of consequence occurred.]

But the "what-if" fears of Y2K paled against the reality of 9/11. Like almost every American, Claudia remembers where she was.

"In my unit, everyone was watching the television in the day room, staring at these two towers that were burning. It took the rest of the day to understand. Were we going to war? Would our families be safe? We discussed all the possibilities. Cheri relied a lot on her faith, but she also had the military background. She was tough."

According to Claudia and other former inmates I spoke with, Cheri was a natural born leader. "Cheri was such a powerful mentor in prison. Everyone went to her. She had an intuitive intelligence for getting at the core of something, a natural talent. And she really cared. She may have had trouble with one or two officers, but most everybody loved her. She is sincere and honest and kind. Everybody gets it. She was the mother hen."

Those traits may have been the reason Cheri was asked to enter a program for drug and alcohol counseling. She talked Claudia into joining her. "We did that for five years," Claudia says, "and after two years of going through the training and counseling together, we were allowed to counsel others."

Cheri was in the small group of women chosen to go through that drug counseling certification program, a first in the prison. According to another inmate in that program, Charlotte Key, only 27 women were chosen from 100 applicants. Seven finished the class and passed the certification test allowing them to counsel others.

"That program changed my life," Charlotte told me. "We were a diverse group. None of us were close friends at first. We had to use 'I' statements. The instructor would pick two facilitators and seat us across from one another. We had to be brave and confront our own truths. We came into prison with resentments and blame. But I never came out of those sessions without a pile of tissues on my chair."

Cerise Laberge was another inmate who joined Cheri and Charlotte in the drug program. "The warden at SVP made it available to women for the first time. We got medical and biological training through the U.S. Navy and UC San Diego. I thoroughly enjoyed Cheri as a human being," Cerise told me. "She had the best stories about her life. About how her mother kept wild animals and Cheri came in drunk once and took the lion for a walk. Who takes a lion for a walk? She was always entertaining, smart, caring and considerate. But her facial expressions could be hard. A sort of chiseled look, somewhat scary. That military bearing could be intimidating. But once I knew her, I loved all of that. And her. She has had a life, that's for sure."

A year into my sentence I was accepted into the Substance Abuse Program. Seven lifers were chosen to participate in the program as residents for two years and upon completion moved into mentor positions. This was the first I learned of domestic violence, battered women's syndrome and PTSD. I was amazed that the information was like my own autobiography. The women in the group had similar experiences and we gave each other the courage to talk about it and the unconditional love to overcome. I learned to live sober.

I started sessions with Sandra, who was the resident psychologist. She believed that I had PTSD and that I had been brainwashed by my father. I began to go back and connect the dots of my past choices and understood myself better. I learned about addiction and the insanity it produces. I also learned to love the women around me unconditionally. I used my story as a tool to give them courage to share their stories. If I was willing to share my past, as sordid as it was, then they could surely share theirs. In transforming my life, I gave hope to the women that it is possible to change. How I wish I could have realized that a long time ago, but I am grateful that I know it now.

Judy: Talk about a radical change. You went from cooking meth in the desert to counseling women about getting clean and sober.

Cheri: I wanted desperately to change. I had a higher power, but I had to be real to get His help. Once I was certified as a drug counselor, I taught recovery classes.

Judy: Were the inmates in the program as eager as you were to change?

Cheri: Not a lot of inmates actually change. It was hard to motivate people. Their arms would be crossed and they didn't want to listen to another inmate. So I started bringing in hardcore lifers for a "scared straight" approach. I wanted to strike fear in these girls, especially those who were getting out. I brought in a lifer nicknamed "Green Eyes" – a tough, Black, loud inmate – who scared the shit out of everyone. She had a real impact. Some amazing people volunteered to come in and work with us. I loved being a teacher. I was good at it. I had earned respect.

Judy: So you were working in the prison, as a certified drug counselor, for the first five years of your sentence. How did that affect your attitude about all the time you still faced?

Cheri: I looked at my sentence as paradigm shifts. 5 year increments. I couldn't think of it as 15 years or, worse, forever. First I am in school. Then I am at work. Then I am on vacation. Then repeat.

Judy: Vacation?

Cheri: I would be granted a few days of "vacation time" between work assignments. But I stayed active on a daily basis. Walking the track to stay in shape, loving the fresh air and the conversation, playing Scrabble, going to church services, going to AA and NA meetings. You know, Judy, if you think about it, everyone is doing life somewhere.

Judy: True. But doing life in prison is especially challenging.

Cheri: I cannot say prison was bad. The hardest thing is missing your family. And it was really hard at times to deal with other inmates. Only about ten percent of them were doing programs. The other ninety percent were in crazy world. That would make me despair at times. I was a bit angry with God: "I have to be surrounded by this insanity, this crap, the rest of my life? NOW you show me what I can be? And now I am trapped."

Cheri was determined to make the most of the opportunities prison offered, and over the years, the commendations and certificates piled up. In addition to completing the drug counseling course, she enrolled in a variety of other courses, from Bible classes to English and History, earning accolades and college credits for her academic achievement. She was voted "Humanitarian of the Year" by the other lifers. But perhaps she took the greatest pride in her Automotive Class.

Cheri: Dad always wanted me to be a mechanic. And I found out I was really good at it. I was the first woman in prison to pass the tough exam that earned me "Master Mechanic" status, which meant – basically – that I could take a car apart and put it back together. I became an automotive teaching aid, earning about 37 cents an hour. I was paid 90 cents an hour for the drug counseling.

Judy: That wouldn't buy much, would it?

Cheri: I used it for toiletries and Top Ramen. My mom would send me money, now and then, and care packages, but I felt guilty about that. She was struggling herself.

The first five years of her sentence were especially tough, despite her determination to stay clean and sober, despite her academic and counseling achievements, because prison is prison and this prison was no picnic.

From a letter to her friend Kit Carson (who saved them all and made them available to me):

"As for surroundings, it's a bad nightmare. I'm in the largest women's prison in the world. There are four separate yards with four housing units on each yard, which house up to 1,000 women on each yard. You don't get to pick who you live with and it can get downright scary. Lots of drugs, homemade alcohol (hooch), fights, rapes, overdoses, intimidation, stealing. Ugly stuff for real. A lot of young gangbangers who don't know what respect is. I do my time carefully. I have nothing to prove to anyone but God and my kids."

The kids. When Cheri went to prison, Michelle was 13, Jason 10. Cheri wrote them letters regularly, but rarely heard back from them. Sometimes many months would pass when she would not get a response of any kind. But Michelle read all the letters, and stored them in a box, which she shared with me. Jason also received letters from his Mom, but never opened them.

"Our mom was always on our minds," Jason told me. "But I was horrible about writing. I mean, what the fuck was she going to tell me?"

Michelle says her mother's imprisonment was always part of her psychological landscape, painful memories that she stuffed away.

"Right after she went to prison, I started going down the tubes. I got on meth, was arrested and sent to the juvenile detention center for a few days. I was on probation, but always running away and acting out. I would ditch school. My freshman year, my GPA was 2.1. By my senior year, I managed to get that GPA up to a 3.5, even earned a scholarship of 10 thousand dollars. But I was still on parole. I was on meth. So I hung out with the wrong people and ended up in bad places."

Sounds sadly familiar.

In prison, Cheri had a lot of time to think about her failures in the parenting department.

From a letter to Michelle:

"I do my best to be grateful for all I have and to be happy. I have a lot of friends in here, but inside I am very lonely and very sorry for the choices I made that have taken you and Jason out of my life. No one or nothing can ever replace either of you. You are so missed by me that it physically hurts me. I know that there is no way I will ever be able to make up for the past and that both of you not being in my life is what I deserve and I accept that. Sometimes I take myself outside of myself and try to imagine being a child with a mother that is locked up for murder. I've done you both so wrong. I hope that you will have the

courage to overcome those obstacles that may keep you from becoming all that is possible for you."

If these heartfelt letters ever had any impact, it was not evident. Those first couple of years of her sentence, Cheri's letters almost always ended with a plea for Michelle and Jason to respond. Sometimes she tried a light-hearted approach: *"I thank God for you and Jason and ask him to protect you and guide you and make you write me! Just kidding. I'm patient and I know you'll get around to it someday (hint, hint)!"* In her next letter, in June 1990, six months into her prison term, Cheri offered them a simple way to respond. *" How are you? I know you have a lot going on sooooo....I made you a questionnaire! Just fill in the blanks and send it back, okay?"*

After a couple of years went by, with sporadic contact, Cheri became increasingly concerned about reports of Michelle's drug use. *"You know all those times I didn't call or come see you? Do you think it was because I didn't care or didn't love you? No way! It was because I was addicted to drugs and ashamed of my life. It was a vicious cycle and you and Jason are scarred because of it even if you don't tell me. I know, because I was plenty scarred myself. Now, I know you love me, so the only reason I can see that you won't write me is that you are on drugs and you are ashamed. I've been there and you are doing the same thing I used to do. So when are you going to get real with me, Michelle? Do you think I could ever love you any less?*

You and Jason got a real raw deal when you got me for a mother. I'm sorry for that more than you could even imagine. I cannot change the damage I've done or all the years I deprived you of a mother because of my addictions. When I gave my heart to Christ, He forgave me every-thing and gave me a chance to start new. I don't take that forgiveness lightly. It's the chance to set things right with you and Jason someday."

Making amends is a key step in recovery programs. Taking responsibility for your actions, saying you're sorry for the damage you caused, while never expecting anything in return is considered a necessary hurdle on the way to solid sobriety. The hard part is that bit about not expecting anything in return, such as signs of forgiveness. Certainly, Cheri was learning that lesson, multiple times. Her apologies, heartfelt and articulate, never ceased in all those years and in all those letters to her children. She got little in return. She understood that this would be a never-ending amends, one that would only be fully realized if and when she were ever released from prison and could make a so-called "living amends" by becoming the mother she had never been before. But for now, she had only the written word and the hope that one day the kids might visit her in Valley State Prison for Women. A slim hope, at least at first. In fact, she was overjoyed when a simple letter would arrive. In the first years in prison, that was almost never.

Becky Mathews, married to Cheri's ex and stepmother to Michelle and Jason, said that before Cheri went to prison, the kids were very angry at their Mom. "They had huge abandonment issues," she told me. "When Cheri was in prison, the kids sometimes refused to write her letters. So I wrote to her and sent pictures."

Jerry Mathews also worried about the kids' reaction to Cheri's prison sentence, especially after Cheri told the family she would be featured in a segment on MSNBC's "Women Behind Bars." "I was watching this show and there is my ex-wife opening up her locker in her cell, telling her story, and she was showing photos of our kids in her locker. And I was pissed. The fact is, their Mom murdered somebody. And there they are, their pictures on TV." Cheri says she never knew Jerry was upset about the TV appearance. In a phone call soon after the show aired, she says, Jason had told her how cool it was, seeing his Mom on television.

Now, Jerry tells me, his feelings have changed. He is glad Cheri has a chance, at last, to actually be a mom to them. But those first few years in prison were intense.

Judy: Those early years, when you had so little communication with your kids, must have been excruciating.

Cheri: Excruciating for them, too. Dealing with a mother in prison, that hurts. Hurt them, hurt me. We are still – all these years later – dealing with their anger and resentment. Jason was just a kid when I went to prison. He didn't owe me shit. I knew it. But I was desperate to communicate with him. My mom brought them to see me once. It was so great. But also painful.

Jason vaguely remembers driving from Nevada to California with his grandmother, Carol, to visit Cheri during her first months in prison. "To this day, I love the smell of sulfur when someone strikes a match to light a cigarette. My grandmother would smoke while she was driving, and I would be trying to sleep in the backseat. I couldn't ride in the front seat, because that was reserved for the urn with Ray's ashes. Her brother, my great-uncle."

That would be the same Uncle Ray who was in prison for murdering his ex-wife and in-laws in Arizona, then escaping in a garbage truck, making his way to California and hiding out at the ranch where Carol was working, before being captured and dying in prison. Good old Uncle Ray. His ashes would ride shotgun for the duration of Carol's life.

Jason says his grandmother was in a wheel chair towards the end of her life after surgery for a bad accident with a horse. "That titanium rod in her leg would set off the metal detector at the prison. She lit that thing up like a Christmas tree. So she always had to get there early for visiting day, to leave time for the personal body search by the guards."

From a letter to Michelle dated December 24, 2001 (2 years after sentencing):

Dear Michelle, Merry Christmas! The phones are broke so I can't call. Did you spend Christmas in Fallon? I miss you tons.

I got a letter from Becky and she said that Jason was kind of quiet and withdrawn after he came to see me. Don't tell Jason I know or that Becky wrote me, but maybe take a minute to talk to him and make sure he is okay. If there is something wrong, he would never tell me. I know how close you are and if he told anyone it would be you.

Even this tenuous connection between mother and daughter was severed in 2003. I asked Cheri why Michelle's collection of letters did not include any from that year. Were they lost, I wondered? No, said Cheri. *Michelle* was lost.

Chapter 26

Do You Know Where Your Children Are?

In 2003, Michelle Mathews was 20 years old and lost in a world of drugs. And then, she was literally lost. As in, disappeared.

"The quick version," she said in a recent conversation with me, "is that I was on meth, partying a lot after I graduated from high school. I hung out with a guy in Fallon who was doing fraud, writing bad checks, so I left our apartment and took off to Sacramento with friends. The boyfriend in Fallon trashed our apartment. Dad went in and cleaned it out, but I had disappeared. I was too ashamed to go back. I ended up on the streets, in the drug world of Sacramento.

Cheri: She's lucky she lived through it. I called Jerry to find out what was going on. 'Go find our daughter!' I was screaming at him over the phone. I was in prison and I was powerless to help. We worked up missing person posters and gave stacks of them to friends who were going to Sacramento. I had so much rage, so much shame and guilt. I was, literally, on my knees, crying to God. And I was so angry at my sister Susie. She had introduced Michelle and Jason to drugs. I wanted her dead. Meanwhile, I was so worried that Michelle is the one who would end up dead. And she came close. She had a horrific experience there – she was raped, sold, drugged.

Michelle told me that she went to "work" for an old guy, a rich accountant, who was very "sketchy." He drugged her, raped her. "Then one day," she says, "I started bleeding and couldn't stand up. I just fell on the floor and begged him to help me. So he dropped me off at the nearest ER and I ended up going to UC Davis Medical Center by ambulance. I was pregnant and had miscarried. Once I was released from the hospital, I remember just wandering around. The cops arrested me and took me to jail for the night. After getting out, I hitchhiked and got picked up by a guy who helped me contact my parents. Dad came and got me and took me home to Fallon. I weighed 80 pounds."

I asked Michelle if that was the end of this horrible odyssey. "No," she said. "I had to go back to Sacramento for my court date. I took a bus there. But I did not go to court. I just wandered the streets again for a while, just a crazy person. I don't remember how long that lasted. Eventually, I got a ride back to Fallon. But I was on drugs again. Meth."

Jason, meanwhile, was struggling through his last year of high school in Fallon. He was also wrestling with drug addiction, the family legacy. The only letter I could find from Cheri to Jason was written at that time.

Dear Jason,

Hey there. I could ask you how you're doing but I have a sneaking suspicion you're not doing too hot lately?

When I was a senior in high school I had an offer to go to the Air Force Academy because of my swim times. At 17 years old, I didn't want to commit 10 years of my life because it seemed like forever to me. So I joined the Army instead because I had to get away from my dad. At the same time, I wanted him to be proud of me. I also didn't believe in myself so I took an easy way out. That pretty much became the rest of my life. I've never been able to handle when things got tough. I would always run. And I self-sabotaged my life over and over again.

I'm sorry you are screwing off your last year in high school. But I'm not disappointed in you at all. I'm sorry because I know you're going to regret the choices you are making later on, but we all grow up regretting something.

I love you no matter what you do or where you go.

Remember one thing. You aren't a failure for falling down, making wrong choices, or for hurting other people. A failure is someone who doesn't get back up. It's never too late to change your direction. I'm proof of that. If I can change my life in prison after all the mistakes and damage I've done, then so can you.

But you have to get off the damn dope. All you're doing is covering up feelings you need to work through sober. That's my prayer for you and Michelle. Be whatever you want to be, but be it sober and free. And you need to come see me, okay?

I love you the best I can. I'm just sorry it wasn't sooner.

Mom

By 2004, five years into her sentence, Cheri at least derived some comfort from knowing that Michelle appeared to have weathered the worst. She was living in Fallon, holding down a job. And she was reconnecting with Cheri.

In a letter dated March 28 of that year:

"Dear Michelle, First I just want to tell you how much your letter meant to me. I shared it with my friends and I read your poem to 125 women in the program and it really touched a lot of their hearts....I really hope you will give me an address to write to you when you get a place. I don't even know where Jason is now and haven't heard from him since his birthday....I'm so glad you are keeping an eye on your Grandma [Carole, Cheri's mother]. I think she is still planning on going to Yucca Valley for a few months. I hope she can stop to visit on the way home. I haven't seen any of you in years and miss you all so much."

The way she ends this letter hints at the beginning of a reconciliation.

"I love you, Michelle.... Thank you for forgiving me."

A few months later, in a letter dated June, 2004:

"Dear Michelle, I hope you are getting my letters. I will try to write more often. I'm still working at the drug program. I teach a Dialectical Behavior Therapy (DBT) class which teaches the girls new skills to deal with their emotions and behaviors. I went through this class with the staff first and it has really helped me with my own emotional rollercoaster.

I am going to write to the District Attorney on my case along with a letter to Davey's mom to tell her how sorry I am for taking her son's life. I just found out I could send it through the D.A. One more step of making amends. It feels scary but if someone killed Jason, I would want to hear an apology."

Christmas week, 2004, Cheri was granted "vacation" time. By this stage of her incarceration, she was keeping a journal. In this entry, she talked about her loneliness and flashbacks.

I was sweeping the floor this morning and I had a flashback of being a little girl anticipating my dad going off on me. I remember how it felt to be waiting for days and trying to stay away from him, waiting and sick and scared. That's how I'm feeling every day lately. The memory was so real, I just broke down and cried. I cried for the little girl and I cried for the big girl who is so fucking damaged I don't know if I'll ever be okay. So, I need a plan for my vacation. Daily exercise, Bible Study homework and classes, journaling and some inner reflection. Clean my locker, wrap Christmas presents, and write letters, and sew. Sounds like a real vacation, huh?

15 years provides a lot of time for mood swings. In both directions.

Cheri: I was very busy in prison. I had a life in prison. I had college, work, friends, exercising, planning groups, teaching. Prison was a godsend. A lot of inmates don't have that much time to get it together. The recidivism rate is high. Acceptance is the key. I had to believe that if I continued to change my life and help other people,

then someday I might have a relationship with my kids. But of course I could not depend on that.

She could depend, however, on the loyalty of the friends she made in prison over the years. "She is remarkable," says Cerise Laberge, who served 20 years, many of them with Cheri. "The life experience she has had! There is almost nothing she has not experienced that does not help others. She has the ability to be soft and empathetic. She has a soft touch for family, but her vigilante stance never left her. How many lifetimes has she lived? Unbelievable."

Judy: I have a feeling I know how you are going to answer this question, but I have to ask. Have you seen the TV series *Orange is the New Black*? Did you relate at all?

Cheri: I saw some of it. Ridiculous.

Judy: Why ridiculous?

Cheri: Killing a guard and hiding his body in the prison garden? So absurd.

Judy: Once again, I think the details are distracting from the big picture here. I am curious about the friendships, the few you could count on.

Cheri: You had to choose carefully. But those friends are still some of the best, the most loyal friends I have ever had.

Cheri's annual photo, taken at Valley State Prison.
Inmates sent these portraits to friends and family.

Chapter 27

Bunkaroos

"If you can survive 11 days in cramped quarters with a friend and come out laughing, your friendship is the real deal"
—*Oprah Winfrey*

11 days on a road trip with a friend is one thing, but how about 11 *years*? Or 15? Or more? Quotable lines about friendship take on a whole new meaning when placed under the microscope of sharing a prison cell for a lengthy amount of time. They don't put sentimental quotations about prison friendships on posters and cards and pillows. "Gay for the Stay" probably wouldn't be a big seller.

Cheri: Women in prison are really into relationships. Women would create their own families in there. But "gay for the stay" wasn't for me. I didn't judge it, but I just didn't want a gay relationship. One woman did approach me. I told her, "Check it out. The last person who had the hots for me, I killed. You do not want a relationship with me."

But deep friendships were a different story. The women Cheri befriended in prison still talk about the difference her empathy and insight made during those very hard years in their "gated community." The women who spoke with me have all been released. They agreed to share their stories.

Susan Mellen

"Cheri is an amazing woman," her one-time bunkmate Susan Mellen told me when I called to talk about their friendship. "I can't think of anybody I would rather be interviewed about."

Mellen is an unusual case. A lot of inmates swear they are innocent of the crime that landed them in prison, but Mellen actually *was* innocent. After serving 17 years of a life-without-parole sentence, the Gardena woman was declared "factually innocent" of the 1997 killing of a homeless man. The Innocence Project took on her case and proved that a witness who testified against her was a notorious liar. That woman's so-called "eyewitness" testimony was the only damning evidence presented at trial. Mellen was 59 years old when prosecutors and a judge agreed that she was wrongly convicted, and that she had received "sub-par representation" by a lawyer who did not even look into the witness' credibility at the time.

While she was still in prison, Mellen says, "I thought everyone believed me when I said I was innocent. I learned later that some of these women just thought I was old and crazy."

Cheri believed her.

Cheri: She was the sweetest, kindest woman. How could anyone even think she could commit murder? She accepted her sentence with such grace. She had been on meth and was grateful that God took care of her. Grateful! She came off as a little ditzy, always in a good mood, doing a little dance, laughing and praising God. That got her through it. We were bunkmates for a couple of years at VSPW. "Bunkaroo," she called me.

"Cheri is the type of woman who is fair," Mellen told me. "If you are fair and honest, she was okay with you. If you played games or tried to be a bully, she wasn't going to like you. She stepped in if someone was being a bully, definitely a peacemaker. She didn't want to fight, but people knew she was capable of going there."

Mellen says she felt honored that Cheri trusted her enough to share her story about Davey's murder. "I always felt I should have told her, 'You were saving your life and your children's lives.' I felt that Cheri knew she and her kids were in danger and she snapped. It makes me cry now, thinking about it. She picked a bad guy, did a bad thing, but she was not a bad person."

Mellen was still in prison when she heard that Cheri got a release date. "I was so happy when I heard the news. Cheri turned her life around. She was on a spiritual journey. I really believe it was God's second chance. I believe God is still with her."

"God's second chance." Nice phrase from a woman who never gave up believing she would get a second chance herself and be vindicated, to boot. In prison, Mellen wrote "freedom" on the bottoms of her shoes because, she said, "I knew I was going to walk free one day."

Cerise Laberge

Cerise Laberge was one of Cheri's cellmates at VSP. Both were transferred years later to the women's prison in Chino and both took part in the California counseling certification program for drug and alcohol addiction. Laberge was convicted of second degree murder and sentenced to 16 years to life, plus one year for a weapons enhancement. She was 18 at the time. She was paroled after serving 20 years of her sentence. Like Cheri, she harbors no bitterness about what happened to her.

"I would not be who I am today if it were not for prison. Arrested in 1994, released in 2016. There were so many women in prison who had killed really bad guys and you just wanted to hug them and say, 'Thank you, because other people are safe because of what you did.' Most women have had massive amounts of abuse. One time, just once, they fought back."

But that knowledge was born from years of counseling others, not from personal experience of abuse. *Her* story was more a tale of wrong guy, wrong time, wrong place. "I had known my boyfriend for about three months when it happened. We were in a car, and I was driving. I thought we were going to his house, but it was his ex-girlfriend's place. He got out and shot her, the mother of his child. Because I was driving, and because we left the scene and I didn't tell on him, I was considered just as guilty of the murder. I was 18, a high school graduate, enrolled in college, the only child of a school teacher. It was so hard on my mother. She did every minute of that sentence with me."

Cerise and Cheri bonded almost immediately in those first years at VSPW and remain friends today. "Cheri has come out, not so much unscathed, but hopeful. She self-sabotaged because of her childhood messages. Somewhere deep inside, she believed those messages and had so little belief in her own self-worth. How many 'fathers' has she had to reinforce that message?"

And yet, says Cerise, Cheri transformed those dark experiences into an ability to connect with others and help them. Cheri never lost that "vigilante stance," she says, but her soft touch for family and those who have suffered made her an outstanding counselor.

Clearly, the same could be said of Cerise Laberge. Just after learning she was to be paroled, corrections officials asked Cerise if she would be willing to go back into the prisons as a facilitator for drug and alcohol counseling. She not only said yes at that time, but she continued to do the work even after she was off parole.

"I am currently going into Chino [prison for women] with the Freedom to Choose program, which teaches that misunderstanding comes through miscommunication. I'm a large group facilitator today, presenting the course material on stage. It's all volunteer work. Empirical studies have shown that the program lowers violent incidents in prison."

Talking to these women had a powerful impact on me. Now, when I have any sort of resentment about anyone or anything, even those that seem oh-so-very-justified, I find it helpful to think of Cerise Laberge and Susan Mellon and all the other women who not only do not harbor resentments from the past, but who work with others to deal with *their* anger and hurt, much of it deeply rooted.

Cerise is now married, living in San Diego. She is still going into prisons, counseling inmates.

Charlotte Key

"I was a year into my 15 to life sentence for second degree murder when I met Cheri. She was so smart. I moved into the honor dorm with her at VSPW and later bunked with her when we were transferred to Chino. We created an honor dorm there, as well, the first ever at that prison. We would play scrabble, and walk and talk. When you first start talking about your case, you are defensive and pissed at yourself because you've done something so extreme, and you realize you weren't equipped with the coping skills other people have. What you have acquired is a series of traumas. Coping skills that kept you safe in childhood come back to bite you in the ass as an adult, they become your downfall."

"Cheri and I talked about things we were denied in our homes. If what we were raised in equals chaos, degradation and abuse, that is what is comfortable for us. Kindness is not comfortable. And if you are raised with the idea that God is this powerful male figure who is also a loving figure, then love means 'you will abandon me and abuse me.' Your abuser becomes your higher power."

Charlotte had no trouble connecting the dots. Cheri's love/hate relationship with her father, she told me, had molded her into something of a "white knight."

"It occurred to me that Cheri could not stand bullies, like her father and stepmother. In prison, she defended weaker inmates against bullies. Now that I think of it, the two men she killed were both horrible bullies."

Charlotte could empathize with Cheri's tough childhood, but rather than memories of a strict, dictatorial father, her memories were of her single mom, raising three girls, all of them molested under her watch. "She knew what was happening," she told me. "My mother sent us off with older men. I was abused by a neighbor from the age of three until I was five. My mother would lock me out of the house. Three years old! People with childhood trauma, like Cheri and me, we were determined that no one else was going to abuse us. We wanted to finally win."

Charlotte's crime sounds like something out of a Coen Brothers movie.

"A 53 year old man in Clear Lake, California, started paying me for sex and supplying me with meth. He was a morphine addict and an alcoholic. I was 29 years old, out of money. I had lost my kids because of my meth addiction and I wanted to get them back. So I told him I would fix up the house before the court inspection. But when I showed up to clean the house before the court date, he was naked, drunk, in a rage. He said, 'Bitch, you're never going to get your kids back.' I snapped."

"Snapped how?"

A pause. "I decided to overdose him on heroin. As I was drawing up the heroin in the spoon, I made that decision to kill him. My hands were shaking. He was drunk and he didn't even realize I was shooting him up."

At this point in Charlotte's story, she skipped past the actual moment of death, straight to the critical issue of body disposal.

"I didn't have a good place to store the body, so I stuffed him in the couch."

"Excuse me?"

"A friend helped me hollow out the couch, a space under the cushions, and we put the body in it. We got a guy to help take the couch away. He put the couch in the trunk of his car and took it to the dump, the landfill."

"So how was the body discovered?"

At the dump, she told me, two police officers happened to be there, unloading trash from their car. "They offered to help this guy lift the couch out of the trunk, and they discovered the body. I ended up taking a deal for 15 to life."

Charlotte and Cheri both worked in the prison's drug and alcohol counseling program. One can see how their stories of hitting

countless "bottoms" --and their subsequent surrender and rehabilitation -- would carry a lot of cred with other inmates. Today,
Charlotte is a counselor for women in a treatment center. The two
of them were best friends throughout their incarceration and
became bunkmates when they transferred to Chino. Living in the
honor dorm at both facilities allowed them some benefits not available to the general population.

From a letter Cheri wrote to her friend Kit Carson: *"Thank you
for sharing photos of your beautiful flowers with me. You are correct,
we don't have flowers. Our unit is the honor dorm so we do have lots
of potted plants in the dayroom, but we are the only unit that does."*
*And from a letter the following year: "Spring is coming soon and you
will be out in your flowers before you know it. I don't have any flowers
here but we do have some grass in front of our unit and I am one of the
waterers whose job it is to keep it green through the summer. I love it."*

This, from the woman who sifted through desert dirt in a desperate search for meth crystals. As her ex-husband Jerry would say,
"the woman is a miracle."

Claudia Chita

Claudia, you may recall, was the cellmate who was almost
attacked by a crazy inmate named India. Until, that is, Cheri intervened. They spent two years in the same cell before they were both
moved to the honor dorm in 2005.

"Sometimes it feels like it didn't even happen to me. Cheri is
so embedded in me, I have dreams about her. I haven't seen her in
14 years. In my dreams, we are always going on some little adventure. There's nothing we didn't talk about. When her kids stopped
calling and writing, Cheri went through depression. Would they ever
forgive her and come see her? She thought about that a lot. I
remember when Jason came. He was the first. She was elated. But
it also brought everything else with it. 'Can I live up to expectations?
What kind of mom can I be in prison?'"

Claudia served 7 years for assault and battery. Now she helps care for the elderly in a community north of San Francisco.

"I wrote to Cheri after I got out, but it was hard. Like a piece of me was still in prison. She was such a powerful mentor, everyone went to her. Her intuitive intelligence helped her go right to the core of something. It was like a natural talent. And she really cared. I believed she turned a lot of girls around. So many wrote to her after they were released. And you don't see that very often. When she finally went to her parole hearing, everybody was pulling for her, even the staff. So many women in there are jaded and cold and heartless, but Cheri was different. She actually challenged herself, she wanted to be a better person."

"I always knew she would not stay in there. She is a soul who should not be caged."

Penny Greer

"Prisoners become excellent observers of life," Penny Greer told me. " Early on, a friend advised me, 'keep your mouth shut, your ears open, and just watch.'"

Penny did that, and was impressed with Cheri from the start. Her first interaction with Cheri was in the law library at VSPW. "I was spending a lot of weekends there, to appeal my life sentence for second degree murder. My public defender had fought for manslaughter. Cheri was working with a paralegal to file a writ to get a new trial. She never did get a new trial, but she wrote a long statement for the parole board and when her parole was granted, she shared her declaration statement with me. We made a copy. When you are reading someone else's timeline, it helps you with your own portfolio for the board. Her statement showed that she was transparent, that she had done the work."

Penny's own story, she says, echoed those of so many women who had been victims of domestic violence. "If people want to know what you're in for, and you say 'domestic violence,' other women get it. I did not share Cheri's story, that dark world of drugs, but other inmates who had that background were especially helped by the fact that Cheri had made her statement to the parole board available to others. Everyone who used that statement as a model was deeply grateful. Me, too."

Penny admits that if she had met Cheri in her past life, her criminal life, she would have had a horrible opinion of her, based on that statement she wrote to the board. "Her life was like a horror movie," she remembers, "and I never watch those. Too scary. But I got to know her in 'our gated community,' and she had so much integrity. She was guarded in terms of her privacy, not exactly an open book, but she was warm and caring."

Penny's husband, an alcoholic who would go into a rage when he drank, died after one particularly bad altercation. "He was coming for me, so I grabbed a knife and I stabbed him. He walked away so I didn't think he was hurt that bad. He was a foot taller than me. Apparently I struck an artery and he died from internal bleeding. My husband's family thinks I should have rotted in jail. But I was paroled on my first board meeting, which was unusual. I'm a 'one-percenter.'"

By that time, Jerry Brown was governor and he was encouraging the release of people who had served their minimum sentence, if they were deserving. And for the first time, the justice system was taking a look at the so-called "domestic violence defense".

Penny Greer's last roommate in prison was a woman named Brenda Clubine, who would go on to establish a program called "Every Nine Seconds," a reference to how often women are abused by violent partners in this country.

The new spotlight on domestic violence would eventually shine on Cheri Mathews. And the consequences of that investigation would crack open her world once again, dredging up those old responses of anger and retribution so enshrined in her father's "code."

As she said, even her bottoms had bottoms.

Chapter 28

Battered Woman's Syndrome

It is unlikely that Cheri Mathews -on her own - would have ever looked into the "battered woman defense" as a way to mitigate her sentence or to help win parole. The very idea that she might be permanently labeled a victim was anathema to her. Even though she had faced the truth of her childhood abuse, as well as the physical and psychological abuse of some of her adult relationships, she had always rejected the idea that she was helpless or weak. A huge part of her recovery from addiction was the honest acknowledgement of her own role in helping to create the mayhem of her adult life.

As someone who has spent months talking to Cheri about the details of her abusive childhood and violent adulthood, I do not think it takes a genius to connect that abusive past to her later behavior. But even as we worked on writing her story together, she balked at my use of the term "abusive father" or "abusive relationships." "Could you just say," she would ask me, "that he 'put his hands on me?'" It was an interesting distinction, I thought, for someone whose father once threatened to chop off her hand with an ax and gave her regular beatings when she was young. And what about all those bruises she had on her neck and arms during her sometimes violent marriage to Jerry Mathews? What about the time a friend witnessed him throwing her across the room, or the time Jerry himself called the police because he was afraid of what he was about to do to her? All those incidents, and more, evaporate in the face of the "code" that was so deeply embedded in her psyche that the very idea of victimhood was repellent.

The idea of participating in an investigation into whether she had ever experienced so-called "Intimate Partner Battering and Effects" was first presented to her by corrections officials. After serving some 8 years in prison, after going through so much counseling and learning to counsel others about honestly facing their demons, Cheri was finally open to the idea that perhaps her criminal behavior might be linked to her abusive past. She decided to trust that a corrections investigator, someone trained to recognize battered woman's syndrome, could help her safely navigate those painful memories.

She would pay for that trust.

First, it's helpful to understand why this particular defense was being embraced so widely by the late 90s. Momentum was building for a more complete understanding of the bias in laws defining self-defense when it came to battered women. A large number of battered women in California prisons were petitioning Governor Pete Wilson for a pardon or commutation of their prison sentences based on the battered woman defense, something that had not been formulated at the time they were sentenced for the murder of their abusers. Brenda Clubine was one of those women.

In what now seems an odd convergence of storylines, I was a reporter assigned by ABC News to cover Clubine's appeal to the Parole Board, an appeal based on a defense that had not existed when she was convicted of killing her husband in 1983. I traveled to the women's prison in Chino, the same prison where Cheri Mathews would serve the final years of her sentence, to attend the Clubine hearing, along with a lawyer from a major law firm who had agreed to take the case pro bono. My research ahead of the hearing led me to believe that Clubine had a strong case. The tiny woman, a former nurse, weighed less than 100 pounds. The husband she killed in 1983, a retired Los Angeles police detective, was more than twice her size. And he was, by all accounts, an abusive monster.

The parole board listened intently as Clubine and her lawyer presented her case, while the prosecutor from L.A. made what seemed a half-hearted argument for keeping Clubine in prison. The basic story, which no one disputed, was that Clubine had suffered repeated (and well-documented) instances of abuse over the years of the marriage. Her husband had stabbed her, broken multiple bones, fractured her skull and torn the skin off her face. These horrendous assaults occurred despite the fact that Clubine had obtained several restraining orders.

In Clubine's words, "Every time he was in violation of the restraining order, whether it was because he vandalized our house or physically beat me, the police wouldn't do anything. They came to my home, they would meet my husband in the driveway and he would just tell them I was being emotional. They wouldn't talk to me. I had to call the D.A. every day for six weeks to get them to file charges."

Among the witnesses testifying at that hearing in a small, crowded room in the prison in Chino were several relatives of the murdered man. But they were there to testify on *her* behalf. One of his sisters said he was a horrible bully, mean and scary, and that Clubine had done the only thing she could do after suffering so many broken bones and beatings. He would have killed her eventually, they said.

Whenever someone asks a battered woman *Why didn't you just leave?*, they are expressing a widespread misunderstanding about this syndrome. Leaving one's abuser is a very dangerous thing to do. Choosing to leave takes tremendous courage. Brenda Clubine was trying to leave.

On the night of the killing, Clubine's husband had come over to the house to sign divorce papers. When her husband arrived, he said he had forgotten the divorce papers in his hotel room. She agreed to go there with him. Once she was in the room, she said, he locked the door and told her she was not going to make a fool of him. He was waving a copy of the warrant issued for his arrest. He told her to take off her wedding ring so nobody could identify her body, then slapped and choked her. He stated that he would kill her and that nothing would happen to him.

Terrified, she promised to drop the divorce proceedings and the charges against him. She then put three Benadryl capsules in his wine and began to rub his back as he fell asleep. Convinced that he meant to kill her once he was awake, Clubine grabbed the wine bottle and hit him on the head, then stabbed him twice before leaving the hotel room. But she didn't believe he was dead. She called his phone for three days, expecting that he would be angry and come confront her. The last time she called, the police answered the phone. She was arrested, convicted of second-degree murder and sentenced to 15 years to life in prison.

When I heard Brenda Clubine tell this story, with her victim's relatives backing her up, I thought she would surely convince the parole board as well.

Not so. The commissioners voted to deny her appeal. I was dumbfounded. I remember interviewing one of those members who voted to deny, doing my best not to show my reaction, but clearly failing to do so by framing my question this way: "So what part of the battered women's syndrome did you not understand?"

While she was in prison, Brenda Clubine founded Convicted Women Against Abuse, organizing meetings inside the California Institution for Women in Chino for battered women who had killed their mates. Over the years, they managed to send a couple of dozen petitions for clemency to the desk of Governor Pete Wilson. Some of those were granted. Clubine herself was released from prison in 2008, and went on to run *Every 9 Seconds*, a non-profit devoted to the prevention of domestic abuse.

So, back to Cheri's story. Does it fit the requirements that define Battered Women's Syndrome? What constitutes abuse? Does it go back in time to include those beatings by her father, those physical altercations with her husband? Is it sustained cruelty and control, underscored with intermittent violence, psychological mind games and gaslighting? Does burying a beloved puppy alive qualify? Nailing the windows shut? Depriving someone of food and sleep? Cheri suffered while living with Davey Hepburn, no doubt, but by the time she killed him, they had been living separately for many months. Not the most classic example of battered woman's syndrome.

She surely knew this. But when a deputy commissioner in the California Department of Corrections suggested Cheri might benefit from a BWS investigation, Cheri was open to learning the truth, even though she knew it might not impact her case. After all, by this time, she was a mentor in the prison drug program, one of the leaders in the prison system, voted Humanitarian of the Year by other lifers. Surely, an in-depth look at the psychology behind her crimes could provide a new window into links between her abusive past and her crime. Whatever the official outcome, it would be another opportunity for growth, another dive into the "rigorous honesty" required for redemption after a life of addiction. An AFGO, as one of my therapist friends would say. Another Fucking Growth Opportunity.

What she had not anticipated was that the person on the listening end of this investigation was not as committed to rigorous honesty. And the blowback was serious.

Chapter 29

A Rashomon Tale of Murder and Abuse

The "Rashomon effect" is named after a 1950 film by Akira Kurosawa, in which a murder is described by four different witnesses, who give four contradictory versions. It's a handy way to refer to the subjective flaws in human perception, memory, and retelling of an event.

Cheri knows something about that.

From a letter she wrote to a Deputy Commissioner of Corrections in 2007:

"Deputy Commissioner K.D. Lushbough,

My name is Cheri Mathews. I met you for a moment during my DOC [Dept. of Corrections] hearing on October 7, 2002. You may recall our conversation. You shared with me that when you read my file it was like reading about your daughter. You shared what happened with your daughter's abuser and the fears of him being released from prison. You said you believed there was more to my case and you ordered an investigation [into Intimate Partner Battering, or IPB] by an investigator from the Board of Parole Hearings. Five years have passed and I was [finally] interviewed. What I believed to be an opportunity to share what actually happened has become a travesty. I have enclosed the findings of the investigator along with letters to her ....requesting a review of the audio tapes and corrections to the statements that are inconsistent with what I actually said. Any assistance you can give would be greatly appreciated.

Most Respectfully,
Cheri Mathews

In other words, Cheri did not initiate this investigation into whether domestic partner abuse might have played a role in killing David Hepburn. But she was open to learning whether the abuse she suffered as a child and in her adult relationships might be important to include in her record when she would face her first parole hearing (still 6 years away). She agreed to a three-hour interview by a Senior Investigator from the Board of Parole Hearings, Cindy Coe. Coe also relied on arrest records, military records, and phone interviews with Cheri's family and friends.

Cheri was so upset with the errors in Coe's final report that she wrote her 33-page autobiography in response, the autobiography quoted so extensively in this book. Coe apparently never bothered to read it, nor did she respond to Cheri's point-by-point refutation of her final report, nor would she agree to Cheri's request for a transcript and/or the original recording of their 3 hour interview. That recording, said Cheri, would support her claim that Coe had written falsehoods in her final report.

Although I had obtained the official report and Cheri's response, I felt it only fair to contact Cindy Coe to see if she wanted to comment. Her comment, via email, was succinct:

"I am sorry, but I have been retired for over 13 years and have no interest in being interviewed regarding this case."

So the official record would have to suffice. This is how it begins:
Deputy Commissioner K.D. Lushbough ordered an Intimate Partner Battering (IPB) investigation pursuant to Penal Code 4801 in reference

to claims by Mathews that she was suffering from the accumulated effects of battered woman's syndrome when this offense occurred.

Maybe this is nit-picking, but when a report *begins* with a falsehood – i.e. that Cheri was suddenly claiming that she had suffered from battered women's syndrome at the time of her crime and had therefore initiated this investigation – well, that's not a promising sign.

Coe also relied heavily on Cheri's original statement to the detectives who arrested her in 1998.

Mathews confessed to detectives that she had taken a .22 caliber pistol out to the desert with the intent of killing herself. While she was there, she decided to contact Hepburn at his residence to discuss their problems. According to Mathews, she confronted Hepburn and asked him why he had told friends that she was a snitch. Hepburn then called her a whore, a bitch and a liar. Hepburn was sitting on the couch wearing only shorts. Mathews told Hepburn he had some of her belongings and she wanted them back. Hepburn told her she was not going to get anything back and he had pre-arranged with the Mexican Mafia to have her killed. He added, "I know the names and addresses of every friend you have. I've already got you handled. Girl, you don't even know what kind of shit you're in." She then just got a sick feeling and replied, "I'm going to be handled? Fuck you, fuck you." She took the gun out of her right pocket and shot at Hepburn until the gun was empty. As the victim collapsed to the floor, Mathews exited the location, frightened he would come after her.

Coe's report again refers to the arrest statement when describing how Cheri returned, with friends, to the scene of the crime and includes a damning quote from one of those friends, Kenneth Streeter.

Streeter told detectives he was "scared to death of her (Mathews)."

Building a case with selective quotes is right out of the Rashomon playbook. From beginning to end, Coe's report casts Cheri in a negative light. Coe implies that this woman who supposedly scared her friends to death changed her story from that earlier police account to fit a narrative more suitable to Battered Woman's Syndrome.

During the March 22, 2007 interview, Mathews NOW [emphasis is Coe's] claims she returned to Hepburn's residence to discuss why he was spreading rumors about her and her involvement with police. Upon her arrival, she believed the Mexican Mafia may have been on the property cooking methamphetamine. She was frightened and nervous because she believed her death may be imminent that day. She recalled Hepburn was sitting on the couch in the living room. As she came into the residence, Hepburn immediately began telling her he could have the Mexican Mafia kill her and no one would know. As he was getting up off the couch, Hepburn allegedly began making threats to harm her children and reminded her he knew where they lived. Mathews claims she panicked and believed Hepburn was coming to get her, she pulled out her gun, and shot him four times. Mathews believes "her triggering event" was when Hepburn began threatening to harm her children. Upon seeing Hepburn fall to the floor, Mathews believed he was faking his death. Fearing Hepburn would chase after her, she immediately left his residence. Mathews later returned, with friends, to determine if Hepburn really was dead and retrieve her personal belongings.

Later in the report, in the summary section, Coe was more blunt.

Mathews' version of how the crime occurred has changed over the past eight years to an account which may attempt to evoke sympathy and understanding as to why she committed the murder. Mathews has changed her story by including the victim's threats against her children's lives, and as he was getting off the couch, she reportedly feared for her life and believed he was coming after her.

Cue the Rashomon Effect. In her lengthy rebuttal to this report, Cheri's very first objection was to the idea that she was suddenly asserting that she shot Davey because he threatened the kids.

"I never said that. [However,] Davey WAS making threatening comments to me and said he knew where my kids were."

This issue of whether a threat to her children played a major role in her split-second decision to kill Davey would circle back when it came time for the parole hearing. Cheri would once again try to make it clear that – while that possibility did upset her – it was not the reason she pulled out a gun and shot him four times in the chest. The Rashomon Effect has echoes, as well, in the initial police report. One might question whether the first statements made by a suspect during a police interrogation are the most accurate of statements. Probably not, especially when the person being questioned is on meth and God-knows-what-else. And yet, Coe relied heavily on that initial report.

Coe also got several key names wrong. She repeatedly referred to Frank Belize, the first man Cheri killed, as "Frank Williams." Getting a victim's name wrong is a rather large blunder. She also referred to the Drug Task Force detective who tried to enlist Cheri's help as "Ray Castenades" and said attempts to locate him had failed. Perhaps that is because his name is Ray Carusco.

If a couple of wrong names were the worst of it, Cheri might not have been so outraged when she read the final report. She outlined each error in her appeals document, requesting corrections be made and that she be provided a complete transcript of the three hour interview. Among the mistakes she listed:

- In talking about the boys next door who had molested both her and her sister, she had never told Coe that those boys vaginally penetrated her. But Coe put that falsehood into the report. When Coe called Susie to interview her for the investigation, that particular lie really upset Susie. Had they been raped by those boys? Had she forgotten or repressed that? "My sister was confused and agitated after Coe called her. I assured her that the investigator had given her the wrong information."

- The way Coe characterized Cheri's relationship with her father, she felt, sounded perverted. "My Dad acted obsessed with me but it was not sexual," she wrote in her rebuttal. "I simply told you that after he hit me, he would say 'I did that because I love you.'"
- "I never said – anywhere or anytime – that I found my husband with another woman."

  This particular error also had a ripple effect, Cheri says. In her letter of protest, Cheri wrote, "My daughter Michelle informed me that Ms. Coe told my ex-husband (her father) that I found him with another woman. I never said any such thing. My ex-husband abused me and that was the reason for our divorce. Ms. Coe ruined any relationship between my children's father and me. This carried to my son Jason who now believes I lied about his father and has not spoken to me since. It took years to build those relationships and it's criminal that Ms. Coe hurt innocent people to achieve her agenda."
- Cheri was also upset that Coe interviewed her ex-husband Jerry Mathews as though he were an expert on domestic abuse, rather than a participant in it. From the report: "Jerry Mathews admits domestic abuse occurred, but does not perceive the abuse to have reached a 'violent' level nor does he believe he, in any way, controlled his wife....It is his opinion the domestic abuse did not rise to the level of violence or control necessary for battered women's syndrome." Cheri found this section especially troubling. "Ms. Coe stated Jerry Mathews' opinion like he is an expert on BWS [battered woman's syndrome]. He is not qualified to give an opinion."

  Coe also implied, in her report, that Cheri had tried to manipulate various witnesses in advance, writing: "On April 11, 2007, this investigator telephonically interviewed

*Jerry Mathews. He indicated he was expecting a call as he
had recently received a letter from the inmate. In that letter,
Mathews reportedly reminded him how 'violent' their
relationship was and asked him to be truthful with his
comments to anyone who might call. Jerry was surprised by
her request and had a somewhat different recollection of
their relationship."*

- Cheri pointed out other misstatements, including this:
  "She was molested when she was a child, and raped as
  a teenager...." Molested as a child, yes. Raped as
  teenager, never.

There's more, but you get the drift. Cheri believes Cindy Coe
was never going to be an impartial listener or an accurate recorder
of events. She explained why when she wrote her appeal to Connie
Axelrod, Chief of Investigations. *"During this interview, Ms. Coe
became derogatory and made several character assumptions based
solely on the fact that I was a drug addict. She made several sarcastic
remarks. When I told her I let some people stay in my house, she said,
'You mean, you had a flop house for drug addicts?' I tried not to take
offense at first. Then I said something about Davey throwing away the
food I cooked and her comment was 'You mean you ate food? Or did
you cook crank?' The next comments were about whether Davey had
teeth, did he pick his face (she was making exaggerated picking motions
with her fingers on her face), then asked me if I had my teeth. I realized
she had already pre-judged me because of my drug addiction. I got upset
and defensive at the end of the interview. Ms. Coe was sarcastic, biased
and misleading in her report. I returned to my room and decided that*

I should take the time to write a history of events so as to put the facts down in a less stressful and judgmental environment."

As I mentioned earlier, Coe never read that autobiography.

Cheri never received a copy of her interview, as she had requested. Coe's report went into the record. These are some of her conclusions, many based on the original police records:

- Cheri's comments to the arresting officers, in 1979, indicate she was not a woman "who was dominated, controlled or fearful."

- The inmate Mathews claims that "the offense occurred as a result of the cumulative effect of the physical and psychological abuse perpetrated upon her throughout her childhood by her father, a former husband, a former boyfriend, and the victim. Based on her life experiences, when the victim rose from his couch, verbally threatening to harm her children, she feared for her and their safety and shot the victim. While some evidence suggests Mathews' childhood and teenage years may have been difficult, her second marriage, her relationship with her boyfriend and the victim do not appear to rise to the cumulative level of control for IPB."

Coe then suggests that Cheri's history of drug addiction, rather than abuse, appears to be the controlling factor throughout her life and that the likely motive for the murder of David Hepburn was *"anger, rage and hostility at her ex-boyfriend's refusal to return her property."*

The investigator's conclusions:

"At the time of the crime, Mathews was not a woman suffering from Intimate Partner Battering and its effects. She appeared to be more like a woman who possessed a strong sense of self, who saw options to improve her situation, and who was attempting to return home to Nevada to be with her children. Several friends describe

Mathews as a determined, confident, and independent woman who 'wouldn't take shit from anyone.' She was able to freely leave her relationship with the victim and had been living apart for six months when this crime occurred. At the time of his death, the victim had no social, economic, sexual, or physical control over Mathews, other than possessing a few of her personal items."

"As a result of this investigation, no mitigation for the victim's murder could be found based on battered woman syndrome or intimate partner battering and its effects. No further investigation is warranted."

Like the newspaper and police reports that described the initial crime, back in 1979, this "investigation" and its conclusions do contain a number of facts. But like those earlier reports, a lot of information is omitted or obliterated. It also contains numerous falsehoods, but anyone reading it would not know that, unless they had Cheri's fact checking efforts alongside the report. If I were a neutral observer, reading about this inmate's history through the lens of a skeptical Parole Boards investigator, I would probably come to the same conclusion: Cheri would have a tough time making a case that she suffered from Battered Woman's Syndrome. She certainly was no Brenda Clubine, and even Clubine had a tough time convincing parole boards she suffered from BWS. Worse, I might also believe the slant of this report: that Cheri Mathews was manipulating the system to qualify for sympathy as a victim of Intimate Partner Battering years after she had killed an unarmed man.

But I don't believe that characterization. Cheri was neither a manipulator nor a liar. So committed was she to the "Code" all her life, that lying was simply not an option. Did she pull an unconscious "Rashomon" on her own history in order to appear more sympathetic? Or did the fact that corrections officials ordered this investigation on her behalf *lead* her to question her own past motives? Or was it a little of both? While her relationship with Davey was jam-packed with psychological abuse, echoing the kind of denigration she had suffered throughout her life, she had never characterized her crime as self-defense. Certainly, the detailed autobiography she wrote as a result of this investigation was brutally honest about her repeated self-sabotage and not a treatise on victimhood. In the end, it doesn't matter, because the impact of the official report triggered a whole new level of trauma.

Cheri: That woman investigator was a bitch. I wrote that bio for her but she never read it. I asked her NOT to call my mother, but that was the first person she called. She wrote that horrible report about me. I wrote and appealed to her.
Judy: What did you say to her?
Cheri: I said 'I want you to call my family and say you lied.' I was so upset about it.

From Cheri's last letter to the Chief of Investigations:
"The most heartbreaking thing of all is my mother. I told Ms. Coe during our interview that my mother did not have the emotional, mental and physical ability to handle an investigation and to not include her. My mother was one of the first people she called. My mother was not there for the phone call but was very worried about calling Ms. Coe back because she felt obligated to return the call. I may never know what happened next – whether my mother called her back or not – because on June 7th, my mother put a gun in her mouth and committed suicide."

Chapter 30

"Even My Bottoms Have Bottoms"

From the **Lahontan Valley News and Fallon Eagle Standard**:
"*Carole Marie Mori Tejeda passed away unexpectedly on June 7, 2007, in Dayton, Nevada. Carole lived in Fallon and was house-sitting for some friends at the time of her death.*"

The obituary for Cheri's mother goes on to describe her colorful life: one of the first women to be a licensed horse rider for races in the state of California, owner of her own restaurant, avid scuba diver, loving grandmother.

It does not mention that she was married six times, that she suffered from bipolar disorder, that she abandoned two of her children at a young age, that her brother Ray had killed an entire family in Arizona and died in prison, or that her oldest daughter was serving 15 years to life for murder. Nor does it mention, understandably, that she had died from a self-inflicted gunshot, saying only that she had "died unexpectedly."

"Carole was like her brother Raymond," her ex-husband Ron Mori told me. "He was a big guy who would just go off in a second, they were both raging idiots in a second." Mori says Carole had given up alcohol and drugs after their son, Ronnie, had died of a drug overdose. Their other son, Kevin, would later die from an overdose of Oxycodone. Despite this family history of untimely deaths, Mori says the way Carole died shocked him.

"I was surprised Carole committed suicide by shooting herself," Mori said. "She never liked guns. She wouldn't even use one for target practice."

Cheri got the news when she was summoned to the sergeant's office at VSPW.

"I remember when her mother died," says Claudia Chita. "She was in shock, unable to cry at first. Her mother was a wild spirit. In fact, they shared a lot of characteristics."

The news devastated Cheri. She felt responsible. And it triggered a crisis of faith.

Cheri: You think you have hit a bottom, but – as I said before – my bottoms have bottoms. When I got to prison, I went from one extreme to another. Diving into Christianity, into courses and accomplishments, wanting to excel in everything. Problem is, I never went through the necessary steps to get there. The reckoning came in 2007.

Judy: The investigation on Intimate Partner Battering?

Cheri: Yes. I unknowingly opened the door and let Ms. Coe into my world, believing that the investigation was in my best interest. Even if unsubstantiated, I believed the report would be unbiased and thorough.

Judy: And instead?

Cheri: The final report was full of lies, of misstatements, and I was furious. The woman called my ex-husband and my mom and told them I had said things I had never said. My mom killed herself and I have always believed that phone call set her off. I had to call everyone and explain that I had never said those things. I wanted that woman to apologize to everyone for her lies. I wrote a detailed disavowal, as well as that autobiography. She never read it, never responded to my letters of protest.

Judy: So what did that do to you?

Cheri: It send me reeling back into my old thought patterns of justified revenge.

Judy: Revenge against the investigator?

Cheri: Yes. I was a mentor in the prison drug program, very active, one of the leaders in the prison system. We were planning a Domestic Violence Day, and I was scheduled to be a speaker. The investigators were going to be there and I was planning to kill her on that day.

Judy: You were planning to kill her on Domestic Violence Day?

Cheri: I was going to snap her neck.

Judy: Jesus. So what happened?

Cheri: I had a real moment of clarity. I could see that there was something really wrong with me. I could stand outside myself and see what was happening, how I was falling into the old thought patterns. I was planning a fucking murder and I was sober! So I got help. I didn't even go to the Domestic Violence Day meeting. Instead, I went to Psych and said I needed help. The therapist put me on Prozac. My life changed. I was no longer obsessing, no longer angry. Within days, I felt like a normal person. Honestly, those meds changed my life. I still take an anti-depressant.

Judy: I must say, I am surprised that no one had ever prescribed anti-depressants before.

Cheri: After my mom's suicide, I was so depressed I wanted to kill myself. Or kill that woman. Medication saved me. But then I thought, 'This is what was wrong with me all my life? REALLY? NOW I change my life, get on the right medication, and I have to live with all these crazies all my life in prison?' I mean, I got kicked out of three junior high schools, and no one ever thought I might need therapy, medication? So, I was better, but I was angry. Angry with God.

And God – a fairly traditional Christian version of a "higher power" in Cheri's definition- had been a key player in her recovery from her addictions and her violent past. Her letters from prison to her daughter, Michelle, were filled with testimonies of her new-found faith, of the benefits of allowing Jesus into your life, of her certainty that God's forgiveness was the only way forward. Michelle and Jason were not receptive to those testimonials, and I have to admit that when I read them, I found the evangelical tone pretty heavy-handed.

From a letter to Michelle, written in 2006:

"I don't know where your life is going, Michelle – but I do know how much our Lord loves you and has a wonderful and fulfilling plan for your life. It's time for a change. Get involved with the church because it is your Christian family that will give you guidance and support. It's so hard to explain how good it is to be sober and be consistent in what I do. It's taken close to 3 years to finish Bible School."

In her prison journal, Cheri regularly wrote down her prayers for a better relationship with her kids:

Dear God, it overwhelms so much, I feel like my heart is literally breaking inside of me. Lord, help me overcome the guilt and shame of the past so I can be persistent in loving Michelle and Jason the best I can today. Guide my words when I write to them and break through the walls between Michelle and I.

Some letters were more exasperation than evangelism, a direct approach that comes across as less sanctimonious. This letter was written to Michelle in 2006, as Christmas approached.

"Please answer me this time. Stop being so selfish and just write a damn letter. Tell me happy birthday, Merry Christmas or F-you, but tell me something, okay?

I love you"

Cheri: After my mom killed herself, in 2007, my faith in Christianity took a hit.

Judy: Beyond your anger at the investigator?

Cheri: Yes. I was enrolled in Bible College. A minister was giving me a scholarship so I could graduate and become a minister myself.

I even studied Hebrew and Greek so I could read some original texts.

Judy: You never do anything halfway, that's for sure.

Cheri: The more I studied, though, the more I realized all of this history was open to interpretation. These Bible stories were all passed down, word of mouth, then written by men. The New Testament was written years and years after the actual events.

Judy: But you kept studying. Sounds like it took more than skepticism to shake your faith. What changed?

Cheri: When my mom killed herself, and my brother died of an overdose, the minister sponsoring me told me they were going to hell, that the Devil had won them over.

Judy: What a cruel thing to say.

Cheri: I told him that was bullshit, that there is no Hell. He started yelling at me, saying "The Devil has you, you're going to Hell!"

Judy: So, not exactly a New Testament kind of guy.

Cheri: I realized that the prison church was just weaponized gospel. I quit.

Judy: What happened to your faith in a "higher power"?

Cheri: I kept studying Jesus' teachings, which I love. But I also studied the teachings of Gandhi and other spiritual leaders. And I realized I had annoyed my friends and my kids with those years of proselytizing about God and Jesus. "Shut up about God, already!" was their attitude.

Judy: So you had your own revelation, so to speak?

Cheri: Yes. My Uncle Chris came to visit me in prison and it turns out he had become a Jesus freak. He was really upset about my decision to get out of the church. And listening to him, I realized how I must have sounded to other people, including my kids. I had idolized my Uncle Chris, but after that, we never spoke again.

Judy: So, this is what you meant by hitting a new bottom?

Cheri: That year was a new surrender. No more extremes. I was centered, at last. Spiritually and mentally.

CHAPTER 31

"We Are All Doing Life Somewhere"

Cheri's final surrender, that final "bottom" and enormous shift from manic to manageable, came in 2007. And the shift brought about a new focus, an acceptance of what might actually be accomplished right there, right then. Even so, the dream of walking out of prison one day was always there, distant but tantalizing.

From a letter to her old Army pal, Kit:

"I plan on attending fiber optics vocational training for a few months, and then I'm hoping by October to be back at the drug program starting drug and alcohol counseling certification. That will keep me busy for another five years. My initial parole hearing is December 2012. It will be pretty rough because I will have to go over everything – my life, my criminal life, psychological reports. It lasts up to 5 hours, and they rake you over the coals. After I go through that, and see if David's family shows up against me, I'll have an idea whether or not I may have an opportunity in the future for a parole consideration. I can't even imagine actually having a chance at freedom again but you never know."

Meanwhile, there was the daily life of a lifer to contend with. Silvia Hedlind, a now-retired community resources manager who introduced NA and AA into Valley State, says she remembers Cheri as one of those inmates who took advantage of every self-improvement program. "She had some slips and falls along the way, I do remember that. But her heart was so good. The staff supported inmates who really tried, and Cheri was one of those. She had a twinkle about her. You could see it in her eyes." Cheri had told me Hedlind was a "huge driving force" behind the programs that helped her at Valley State. The Long Termers Organization – LTO – for one. "You had to be clean and sober for 10 years or longer," says Hedlind, "and you had to be 'write-up free' – no serious infractions. The Toastmasters program was popular, too. The ladies gave speeches that would knock your socks off."

In 2012, Cheri graduated from the course certifying her as a drug and alcohol counselor in the state of California. She was cheered on by friends Jackie Banovich and Claudia Jacobs, who traveled to Valley State Prison for the ceremony. Cheri was named Salutatorian.

Perhaps the greatest gift of the last years Cheri spent at VSP in Chowchilla, before she was transferred to the Women's Institute at Chino, was her renewed connections to her children. In a letter to Kit, December 28, 2009:

"*The visit was an amazing miracle. They have both been sober for a year. Michelle saved all year and paid for the trip and hotel and food. Jayde [Cheri's first grandchild, Jason's oldest daughter] is precious and perfect and we hit it off right away. It was so wonderful it was surreal and I'm so grateful to see them in their right minds, healthy and happy. Jason and Shannon married March 12th and she is beautiful. God has shown me more grace than I could ever hope for. They are cutting over half of the programs here next month but automotive has survived the first round, so I am still "employed." I'm super busy with work, college and new self-help groups that I will be facilitating. All good stuff. We will try to offer groups and workshops every day to make up for most people being unassigned.*"

In 2011, however, she received a visit she had neither expected nor wanted. She wrote about it in a letter to Kit:

"*Some detectives came to see me from San Bernardino a few weeks ago about the first shooting that happened in my house in 1993. I was never charged for it and now they have re-opened the case. If they charge me I will have to go to county jail in San Bernardino and possibly face a trial. I can't go back and change anything, so I will deal with whatever comes. It will be good to have it resolved, either way. As for the case with David that I'm going to the parole board about – I have written to David's family before apologizing for what I did. Whether that helped them heal, I don't know. With this other case still unresolved, it doesn't make much difference. I'm not leaving anytime soon. My parole board hearing will be more like a progress hearing for now. I have changed my life and that's all I have the power to do.*"

And so it would go – alternately hoping the parole board would give her a chance to one day walk out of prison, then despairing of it ever happening. And always, in the back of her mind, the murder of Frank Belize simmering as an open case in San Bernardino. But she prepared, anyway. Silvia Hedlind created a mock parole board, so inmates could practice ahead of time. "We'd tell them what they did right and what they did wrong," she says. "Cheri was in that. A lot of those ladies were good people. I thought Cheri was a charming human being."

Charlotte Key, Cheri's last bunkmate and one of her best friends, remembers rehearsing for the parole board. "One of us would play the part of a board member and ask tough questions:

'Why did you go there that day? Why did you take the gun with you?'

'Because I wanted to scare him.'

'Cheri, loaded guns are used to kill people.'

And she would break down and talk about her anger. How she had fixed up his house, how he had abused her. And then she finally admitted, 'I wanted to win.'"

Charlotte says she understood what Cheri was talking about. It might not fit the legal definition of Battered Woman's Syndrome, but it was a motivation abused women understand. "We were people who had serious childhood trauma. *We wanted to finally win.* No one else was going to abuse us."

Rashomon, redux.

One of the groups Cheri became involved with during her years leading up to the parole hearing was the Mental Health Group, where she acted as a co-facilitator with Sandy Schulte, the senior psychologist at the mental health department in Valley State Prison. In a letter Schulte wrote on behalf of Cheri in 2012 to the Board of Parole Hearings, she talked about the amazing transformation Cheri had gone through since she first arrived in prison.

"Then, she was drug addicted and living in chaos and violence. Today, she exudes a peacefulness that was obtained with personal confrontation and hard work. She has struggled with daily prison life, the loss of family members, and family tragedy. These experiences have broken many inmates, but in Ms. Mathews' case, she has found ways to strengthen herself despite these challenges.

She is very bright and has done, and continues to do, tremendous work on her personal growth. One way she did this was to participate in the writing projects of the psychotherapy group we were involved in. She is very articulate and contributed powerful poetry to the project that has resulted in a book co-authored by this writer, **We Are All Doing Life Somewhere.***"*

That book, published by Balboa Press in 2012, written by Lori Williams and Sandy Schulte, is still available on Amazon. The poems were written by four women serving life sentences, over a period of several years. Even though I had been immersed in Cheri's story for months, her contributions to this slim volume of poems blew me away. My favorite is her first, a rumination on fear, the emotion that propels every addict.

Fear of not fitting in
picked up the first joint
a taste of belonging
was the lime in my tequila
licking the salt off his neck
wasn't I the cool one
Fear
driving me, riding me, owning me
taking me to new and lower levels
looking for the way out of my own skin
Fear of being afraid
picked up the gun
loaded it with the shame
of what I let you do to me
Fear
picked up the empty casings
and pretended I didn't kill you
Fear of myself
Picked up the pen

and signed my confession
how cool am I now

I couldn't help but think of the legal parameters for Battered Woman's Syndrome and for Intimate Partner Battering and how limited those boundaries are. Cheri's whole life, from those terrifying days at home as a young girl, idolizing a flawed father, to her adult days of addiction and crime, when she continued to seek approval of deeply flawed and psychologically abusive men, added up to years and years of the "fear of being afraid" and hiding her shame beneath the armor of bravado.

The co-author of the book, Sandy Schulte, writes about the various developmental stages the four inmates went through during the years they worked together. "In the initial stages," she writes, "survival and adjustment were paramount, while later on issues of 'who am I' and 'what's this all about' came to the forefront. We watched them struggle to negotiate the dilemma of responsibility and self-acceptance in spite of their previous actions. We watched them negotiate these issues bravely and courageously in spite of feelings of fear and vulnerability. The poetry illustrates how four women 'stared down their demons' in order to become more fully integrated people. I think that the process reflected in the poetry is not unlike what we all go through as we struggle to evolve. After all, we are all doing life somewhere."

Another poem Cheri wrote for this book highlights that internal struggle:

The little girl is soft, pliable
Eager to be molded into the likeness
Of her heroes
Her role models are unaware of their power
Power to create outside the womb
Demanding and short-sighted
Their expectations are unrealistic

For they are but babes themselves
Their choices create her path
Shame, fear, confusion, anger
Constant companions that eventually
Integrate into her ego, her line
Of defense and eventually her downfall
Now on her own path, she sheds the
Accumulation of other people's baggage
She re-invents herself and becomes herself
Freedom!

It's interesting that Cheri uses the third person when she writes about her childhood, because the poem in which she comes to grips with her crime is in the first-person, the evolved voice of someone who seeks redemption but who knows these amends are, brutally, never- ending.

What gives me the right to be sane
When it cost you your life?
What kind of Black Magic Voodoo crap
Not to see how twisted I was?
Now I see and I'm forever changed.
Here lies the unacceptable quandary
I took your breath and learned to breathe.
....
I, a thief of life, waking everyday
You, forever sleeping
Lifting my face to feel the sun's warmth
You, forever cold
I'm saved and condemned
Walking a wire between my own heaven and hell
Seeking balance of who I was and who I am
Accepting that I cannot make this right, ever.

Making it right, of course, is impossible when talking about taking someone's life. Making amends, on the other hand, is not completely out of the realm of possibility. In preparing for her first appearance before a parole board in 2012, Cheri prepared a victim impact statement. The victim, in the narrowest sense, was David Hepburn. But like everything Cheri does, this statement was meticulous and comprehensive. In 12-step recovery groups, Steps 8 and 9 are considered vital to becoming "rigorously honest" about the "wreckage of your past." Step 8 requires making a list of all those you have harmed. Step 9 calls for making direct amends to them all, "except when to do so would harm them or others." Cheri's victim impact statement reads like an in-depth dive into a bottomless pit of past wreckage, a road map to rigorous honesty.

Victim Impact Statement -Mathews W78136

"Beginning this with the murder of David Hepburn would be incomplete, so I believe it is necessary to first acknowledge the many other individuals I victimized. In each instance, I had opportunities to see the error of my ways, make amends and make the changes in my life to insure no more harm would come by my hand. The failure to acknowledge these individuals during my life led me to continue down the criminal path that ended with David's death."

Cheri then proceeds to list just about everyone she had ever harmed, starting with young girls she had fought with in school and those who were not even aware they had been victims.

"My dad and my uncle never knew I stole from them, but it nevertheless impacted them financially and if they had found out, it would have hurt them deeply."

Some of her most poignant "amends" are to members of her family.

- "I was a terrible role model to my brothers and sisters. I continually thought only of feeding my addictions and justified involving them in my dangerous and destructive lifestyle. Because I wasn't the one who actually got them started on drugs or alcohol, I believed that my using had no influence on them, and I deliberately ignored my responsibility to them as their big sister..... Both of my brothers killed themselves by overdose. My sister Susan is still lost in her addiction. I contributed to their demise by not interceding in their self-destructive behaviors when I had the opportunity. I may not have been able to change things but I could have been a caring and loving influence. I did attempt this after my incarceration but, by then, I was not credible or effective."

- "The men in my relationships were victimized by my codependent and addictive personality....both Jerry and Joey put up with my gambling even when it cost them money to cover the bills I was unable to pay. I was abused by Jerry, and I don't condone it, but I can see today the part I played not only in initiating physical violence with my anger and control issues, but also by continually returning and reinforcing the abusive behaviors."

- "My mother was my victim through the years all the way to her suicide. I took advantage of her guilt over leaving me and allowed her to support me in prison even though I was aware she was struggling financially, mentally and physically. I opened up my family and friends to the I.P.B. investigation that caused them al unnecessary emotional distress that ended with my mother's death."

- "I have sold and manufactured drugs and there must be hundreds of people, many of them children of my customers, who have been directly and indirectly harmed because of my decision to distribute harmful and illegal substances. There are countless people who have robbed and harmed others to pay me for their drugs. Mothers have deprived their children of food, shelter and emotional support because they were scraping together whatever they had to pay me for drugs. My customers have suffered addiction, homelessness, job loss, and untold psychological and emotional pain."

When I read this last bit about all the harm she had caused by manufacturing and selling drugs, I could not help thinking about all the corporate "dealers," aka Big Pharma. I thought about the Sackler family, about the billions of dollars they had raked in from the manufacture and wanton distribution of opioids. *They* would never have to sit down and write a victim impact statement nor would they spend a day in prison. True, they had to pay damages to settle massive lawsuits while their lawyers wrote up careful statements aimed at skirting personal responsibility. Thousands upon thousands of addicted people in this country died of opioid overdoses, but the Sacklers are still living the quintessential "lives of the rich and famous." At least Cheri took ownership of her part in the methamphetamine mania that impacted so many lives, including the lives of those closest to her.

– "My own children grew up with an alcoholic, drug and gambling addicted mother who finally left them altogether for drugs and men. I put them in continual danger by driving with them while intoxicated and by having them exposed to dangerous people. I have broken their hearts more times than I can bear to recall....They have been ashamed, embarrassed, angry, and hurt by the very one who is supposed to honor, protect and love them beyond her own life. They will carry those scars for life."

Cheri also touches on the killing of Frank Belize. She knows, as she is writing this, that the parole board will read it. She knows, too, that it is an open case that could eventually circle back to swallow her up.

- "Someone requested this case to be reopened in 2010 and it may have been his daughter, now grown up and looking for answers about her father. I do know the event traumatized my children and my friends in the house. My friends buried a body because of me. They helped clean up a horrific scene because of me. They have had to make several statements to the police and relive the event. They will carry that memory for the rest of their lives."

After pages and pages of these soul-searching and soul-searing confessions, Cheri finally gets to the murder of David Hepburn, the crime that has landed her in prison, the crime the parole board will focus on.

- "This long history of criminal thinking and behavior, addiction, selfishness, impulsivity, irresponsibility and disregard for society and for human life, along with a lack of accountability, led to the murder of David Hepburn. When I first met David, I was absconding on my parole from Nevada....David promised to get me the equipment and chemicals I would need to manufacture methamphetamine again. Manufacturing had given me power, money, and control (I believed) over my own life. I wanted that back. Agreeing to fix up David's place was more about getting back what I had lost than it was about any feelings for David, at least in the beginning. Although I came to care and (what I thought was) love David later, I always had selfish motives for being there. It was a place to live, a place to have my children come visit, It was drugs and it was a relationship, no matter how twisted.....He died in his addiction. I deprived him of any chance of redemption for his own life. The more I rehabilitate, the more intensely I realize what opportunities I took from him."

This last part surprised me. It seemed a radical departure from all the conversations Cheri and I had about her life on that remote ranch with that horrifying, frightening, psychopath. But then I realized that her attempt to "own her part" in the events that led to Davey's murder actually revealed a level of maturity in recovery that a lot of people would be hard-pressed to achieve. At the most basic level, much deeper than the legalese of an official victim impact statement, she managed the difficult job of letting go of the anger and rage she had felt for David Hepburn. At least she attempted to let it go. But it was also self-serving, in the best way. As Saint Augustine (purportedly) once said, "Resentment is like drinking poison and waiting for the other person to die." In her statement, Cheri basically said the same thing, in her own words:

"David had an ex-wife and six children. Those children grew up never knowing their father. I took that right away from them. Once again, it is grief mixed with justifiable anger that can bring bitterness, hatred and a desire for revenge. I know how damaging that can be and how it can play out throughout life."

David's ex-wife and children had reportedly been hiding from him, having fled the scene before Cheri showed up. Even so, she admitted, she had no right to erase any chance, however remote, that those relationships might have changed with time.

Cheri did not stop there. She included all the peripheral players, as well.

"The first victims after David's death were Kenny Streeter and Bonnie Worden. I involved them in a murder. They helped me for no other reason than friendship. There was no gain to be made by either one of them. Kenny actually saw David's dead body and was traumatized."

"The first responders (EMTs, police, firefighters) to the scene of the crime were exposed to the trauma of a shooting death. They carry those

memories for a lifetime and they brought those events home to their families. I contributed to that."

"The owners of the property David lived on now have a property where a murder took place. There was blood to be cleaned up and they had to find new tenants."

"My ex-husband Jerry raised the children on his own. He had to answer very difficult questions, and witness their hurt and confusion over the things their mother had done. He was subjected to an IPB investigation and once again was shamed because of me. I know that he is deeply affected by the emotional turmoil my children are suffering now because of the possibility of my release. He and I have made amends to one another, yet I am still impacting his life."

Judy: Did you ever make amends to David Hepburn's family?

Cheri: I was allowed to send a letter to his mother. I never got a response.

Chapter 32

"Your Statement Gives This Panel Pause"

Cheri's victim impact statement was no aberration. She had always been honest, even when it might have come back to hurt her. Confessing to the killing of Frank Belize is a prime example. But facing a parole board for the first time was a whole new arena, one with rules and regulations and huge consequences.

The "Lifer Parole Process" is meticulously outlined by California law:

"Inmates serving life sentences become eligible for parole hearings by statute one year prior to their minimum eligible parole date (MEPD). At the hearing, the panel considers all relevant and reliable information in the individual case in order to determine whether the inmate is suitable for release. If an inmate is found unsuitable for parole, statutory law requires that the next hearing be set 3,5,7,10, or 15 years in the future."

In other words, if you miss the brass ring this time, it's not going to come around for *at least* three more years. That's pressure.

Some of the factors showing suitability for parole, as outlined in the California Code of Regulations, include signs of remorse, motivation for the crime, institutional behavior, and whether the inmate suffered from Battered Woman Syndrome or Intimate Partner Battering at the time of the crime.

There's more, but you get the picture: the inmate is walking through a mine field of criteria that could backfire with one false step. Even if the inmate wins a release date from the two commissioners present (one is appointed by the governor, the other is a civil servant), the governor can reverse the decision within 90 days.

Judy: Were you optimistic about the possibility of parole? Jerry Brown was governor then. And he was trying to reduce prison populations.

Cheri: We all knew Jerry Brown was bringing a change. I fell into that perfect timing of Brown coming into office and ordering the parole board to release people who had good records and had done their minimum time. I was doing 15 to life and I was coming up on 15.

Judy: And?

Cheri: As it turned out, at my first board hearing the IPB investigation came back to haunt me.

That first board hearing took place October 24th, 2012, at 2 P.M. at Valley State Prison in Chowchilla, her home since 1999. The presiding commissioner was Jeffrey Ferguson, the deputy commissioner was James Martin. The only others attending were Cheri, her attorney Robert Budman and the Deputy D.A. who was there to argue against release.

Cheri was asked about everything, from her troubles as an adolescent to details about the murder of David Hepburn. Even though I have already quoted extensively from the transcripts of the hearing, the intensity and depth of the grilling are difficult to capture.

Why, asked Commissioner Ferguson, did she use so many substances?

"I remember when I first began using drugs. It wasn't even a question. I wanted to fit in. I found an escape from my home life which I found unbearable with my father. I felt more powerful, pretty, had friends. I didn't have much self-esteem. And I did not feel equal to the kids that were doing better, that were doing the right thing. And I continued in that lifestyle throughout my life."

Early in the session, Ferguson brought up the issue of domestic violence. Was that a factor, he wondered, in Cheri's relationship with David?

"There was domestic violence. Yes. It was not physical. It was psychological, emotional, financial."

After she described the details of that abuse, right down to Davey's burying her puppy alive, Ferguson asked that never-gets-old question:

"And why didn't you just leave?"

"I did. I left several times and I kept coming back."

"At the time of the commitment offense, were you still in that relationship, or had you been separated?"

"No. We'd been separated probably six months."

On the night of the murder, Cheri told the board, Davey sent her into a rage with his taunting and veiled threats:

"He was being verbally abusive to me, but he did not threaten to harm my children. He said 'I know where your children are.' That was what he said. David used to do like this running dialogue with me, in a real low voice, calling me names, telling me he was going to do things like, you know, gut the puppies. Or he would tell me what a shit I was. And it was that kind of tone where I would start crying and feel powerless with him. Like he could do what he wanted to me, and there was nothing I could do about it. That was the type of dialogue that was going on. It wasn't anything that warranted me killing him. There was nothing that he did. He came up off the couch. He didn't have a weapon. There was nothing. It was me.... He had betrayed me, putting a snitch jacket on me. It was bad enough that he had abused me and that I had left with nothing, and then I tried to be loyal to him. So I wanted revenge. I wanted him to suffer the way I believed he had made me suffer."

Reading this brutally honest testimony in the official transcript of that hearing, I was aware of Cheri's need to defend against what she knew was already in the record: the IPB (Intimate Partner Battering) report. Her lawyer made a point, in wrapping up the session, that Cheri had never claimed to be a victim of battered women's syndrome.

Attorney Marcia Randle:

"The only reason she wrote that narrative was at the recommendation of a Commissioner who recognized symptoms of that syndrome. Although she was not diagnosed as suffering from this Battered Women's Syndrome, the domestic violence dynamic is pretty evident here. A long time ago, Ms. Mathews equated love with torture, threats, this person putting a gun to her head. And to someone who subscribes to a violent and dysfunctional lifestyle at that time, to that person, this is love. That is what love is. But through her domestic violence programming, she is now able to recognize how unhealthy that kind of relationship is. And she's able to articulate the warning signs of a potentially abusive relationship. That's something she couldn't do back then. And I just want the panel to recognize that 180 degree difference in her view of that unhealthy relationship."

But the parole board was not convinced. In his concluding remarks, the commissioner quoted directly from that IPB report written by Investigator Cindy Coe:

" 'Hepburn allegedly began making threats to harm her children and reminded her he knew where they lived. Mathews claimed she panicked and believed Hepburn was coming to get her. She pulled out her gun and shot him four times. Mathews believed her triggering event was when Hepburn began threatening to harm her children....Mathews' version of how the crime occurred has changed over the past eight years to an account which now may attempt to invoke sympathy and understanding as to why she committed the murder. Mathews has changed her story by including the victim's threat against her children's lives.'"

"And that does give this panel pause."

And a "pause" is all they needed. Clearly, the IPB report was in the back of their minds from the moment the hearing began. Few lifers serving time for murder are paroled on their first try, and anything that undermines that "suitability for parole" definition carries a lot of weight.

And, just for good measure, the board commissioner threw in a troubling observation of his own:

"Today you claimed you went back to the scene to see if he was really dead. That statement does tend to stand in stark contrast to what actually did occur. What did occur was you returned to the residence and you cleaned up the crime scene by picking up the expended shell casings. You retrieved the letter that you had written to the victim that portrayed you as a snitch. You also robbed him of his personal property."

A parole board hearing is not a trial, where statements like that can be parsed and rebutted by the defense. This was a summation, a reason for denying parole.

"You have come a long way in your development. You have started to form insight in your ability to accept full responsibility for your behaviors. But you still stop short in some areas. And when you minimize and when you fail to identify your true intent, what you're doing is accepting less than full responsibility for your behaviors."

Reading this conclusion, after absorbing the brutally honest testimony and acceptance of responsibility by Cheri during this hearing, I was reminded of the anger I felt at the Brenda Clubine hearing. Were these people hearing the same thing I was hearing?

Cheri: That first parole board, they basically said "No WAY you are getting out." They also brought up the open murder investigation into the death of Frank Belize.

Judy: So you figured it would be at least three more years before you got another shot at parole?

Cheri: After that first board, I gave up hope of ever getting out. That's why it was so shocking when I learned, less than a year later, that I would be appearing before a second parole hearing. I mean, that just doesn't happen.

Chapter 33

"Show Me How Big Your Brave Is"

In 2012, California closed Valley State Prison for Women in Chowchilla and transformed it into a men's prison. Some of the women, including Cheri and her bunkmate Charlotte, were transferred to the California Institution for Women in Chino, or CIW. It houses about 14-hundred inmates.

Cheri: That was a lucky transfer.

Judy: Why? What was different?

Cheri: We had two-person cells. There were a lot of lifers there. The Manson girls had been there forever. Leslie Van Houten was my English teacher.

Judy: Was that weird?

Cheri: No. She's just another inmate. She never talked about her crime. But she was very angry and bitter at the parole board.

Van Houten was 19 years old when she joined the Manson Family. Now in her 70s, she has been serving a life sentence at CIW for a pair of brutal 1969 murders and conspiracy to kill five others. While in prison, she earned a bachelor's and a master's degree. She has had numerous appearances before parole boards. In the beginning, as you might expect, she was turned down. Later, when 4 separate boards were in favor of her being paroled, Governors Jerry Brown and Newsom reversed the decisions. No governor wants to be the linked to the release of any former member of the Manson family. Politically incorrect, to the max. But it serves as a reminder to all lifers– if they needed one - that a chance at parole can turn on the whims of three people: the two commissioners at the hearing, and the governor-du-jour. And that invisible fourth player: politics.

California is one of only three states where the governor has the final say on decisions by state parole boards. Governor Jerry Brown took office in 2011 and during his first two and a half years in office, he approved parole for 82% of the more than 1500 lifer cases presented to him by the parole board. He reversed their decisions less than 20% of the time (i.e. Van Houten). That's a sharp contrast to his predecessor, Arnold Schwarzenegger, whose reversal rate was 70%.

As of 2013, more than 26,000 prisoners in California, one in five, were serving life sentences, which was the highest percentage of lifers among state prison populations.

After Cheri's first chance at parole was rejected, she was resigned to the possibility that she might never get out of prison. But at least she was in a better prison.

Cheri: As soon as we got there, Charlotte and I asked if we could create an honor dorm like we'd had at VSPW. It was a new concept at Chino, but they let us do it. We had our own wing, and we were allowed to paint it and make it nice. There was lots of resentment from some of the other inmates, but our attitude was "Hey, too bad." Living in an honor dorm really makes it more bearable. There's less violence, less drugs.

And then, the greatest gift of all: word came down that Cheri was being called before a second parole board, barely a year after she had been denied parole by the board at VSPW.

She was stunned.

Cheri: I didn't understand it. NOBODY gets called back. I had not requested it. Nothing. I had steeled myself for a life in prison. I went into it a bit half-assed, since I had not really prepared for it. I had a public defender and HE wasn't ready. We just did our best. It was strange, because this hearing had a whole different vibe. The commissioners were even joking, "Have you ever seen Breaking Bad? Because it has nothing on you! You should write a book!"

She was determined to be as honest and forthright as she could be. The year that Cheri became eligible for her second board appearance, 2012, she heard a song that took up residence in her brain and gave her strength. Sara Bareilles' "Brave" is an anthem for all those who have been afraid to escape whatever "cage" they are in, to finally "speak your brave." Since copyright laws prohibit our printing the lyrics here, we would encourage readers to take the time to listen to the song. It's powerful.

Cheri had this anthem for encouragement, but she also had the backing of all those people who wrote letters to the parole board on her behalf. Prison staff, fellow inmates, family. Some, like daughter Michelle, wrote for both hearings.

"I would like to speak from my heart in this letter. My first letter I hope gives insight and I would like to add upon that. When my mother went in front of parole last year, the hope we felt was as much a blessing as it was a trial. My family and I knew the chances of my mom being granted parole was slim, since it was her first time to board but that does not stop the hope that springs inside. Thank God I have hope that one day I will have my mom home. She is a different person than the one arrested 15 years ago. My mother is now an intelligent, compassionate, humble, loving person and I am proud to be her daughter."

Her ex-husband, Jerry Mathews, also wrote a parole support letter:

"Our children have so missed their mother growing up. They do remember the good. I remember the good. We do believe you will look

hard into the person she has become now...for the sake of my children and grandchildren."

Even Jerry's wife, Becky, weighed in. Cheri says that letter impressed the board.

"While Cheri has caused much suffering and strife in her life, she has also suffered many losses herself. She has lost two brothers, her mother, her stepmother and a very close friend. Not to mention she was not present at the marriages of both her children and the birth of 3 (soon to be 4) granddaughters. I do believe Cheri to be a changed woman.... She went so far as to send a card to me, acknowledging and thanking me for being there for her children when she was not able to be."

A number of former inmates wrote letters, as well, describing how Cheri had supported them through the darkest hours of incarceration. Palma Kuykendall wrote twice – and told me she sent one of those letters by certified mail to Governor Brown's office.

"Cheri literally saved me from the first time an inmate who tried to harm me [at L.A. County Jail]. She put herself in front of me and stood up to the other woman and diffused a violent confrontation with reasoning. That woman backed down and never bothered me again.

I had not seen Cheri for 14 years. Last year I visited her in Chowchilla. I can honestly tell you I was shocked at what I saw. The angry, drug-addicted woman was gone. In her place stood a vibrant, healthy, enthusiastic, beautiful woman."

Even with all that support – more than I have included here, of course, Cheri was not optimistic about this second bite at the apple. But she knew that "rigorous honesty," the bedrock of recovery, was the only possible route to redemption, whether it came behind prison walls or in the form of freedom. So one of the first issues she had to address in this hearing, at CIW on April 29, 2014, was the question of whether her victim, David Hepburn, had threatened her children. The previous parole board had made it clear, on the record, that they thought she was trying to look sympathetic with that claim, something the Intimate Partner Battering investigator had also concluded. At this hearing, Cheri came clean. From the official transcript:

Inmate Mathews:

"I believe if there was anything stated about my children being threatened, that was inaccurate and I lied."

Presiding Commissioner Brian Roberts:

"Okay. So what do you mean by that?

Inmate Mathews:

"David did not mention my children."

Commissioner Roberts:

"David did not mention your children?"

Inmate Mathews:

"No, he didn't."

Commissioner Roberts:

"So when you shot him it wasn't about threatening your children?"

Inmate Mathews:

"No, sir."

Commissioner Roberts:

"Because you've said in the past it was."

Inmate Mathews:

"I did."

Commissioner Roberts:

"When did you change the story?"

Inmate Mathews:

"I changed the story in 2001. I did a writ. I filed a writ [of habeas corpus, aimed at presenting new evidence, which was denied] and I believed at that time I was never going to get out of prison if I didn't get out of my original plea and get a lesser charge. Grey Davis was in office back then. And that was the general consensus, that we weren't getting out of here. I got scared and filed a writ. And in

[my new statement] about the crime, I added that he had threatened my children and that that was a triggering event. And I carried that lie through to my first hearing. And I regret that."

Commissioner Roberts:

"Because that was part of the problem for the last Parole Panel. Different stories, you know. When did you undo that statement? When did you decide to say, actually, he didn't threaten my children?"

Inmate Mathews:

"I really wanted to do that at the last hearing. And I just got embarrassed and shameful and I didn't say it completely. I said, 'Oh, well, he didn't really - he said he knew where my kids were but he wasn't actually threatening my children. I mean, I was trying to clean it up and I didn't clean it up all the way. Because it wasn't there at all."

I wasn't in the hearing room, of course, but I can only imagine how stunning that admission must have been. In fact, it wasn't until I read the transcripts of the hearing myself that I was aware that Davey never made an implied threat against Cheri's kids.

Judy: I have to say, when I read that in the transcript, I was shocked. I had believed, all along, that Davey had threatened your kids, simply by saying that he 'knew where they lived.' And you were making that up?

Cheri: It was the last piece of denial. Subconsciously I wanted there to be a reason, other than 'I wanted to kill him.' So I lived with my own lie for years, wanting it to be true. When I told the second Parole Board I had lied, I thought it would be the end. I thought they would never grant parole.

Judy: So why did you admit it was a lie?

Cheri: Because I had to. Nothing means nothing if I can't tell the truth. It was very scary. But what's all this work been for if I can't be honest?

From the official transcript:

Commissioner Roberts:

"So why is it, do you think, that David had to die?"

Inmate Mathews:

"Because I believed at that time that he had hurt me, abused me, used me, thrown me away, because he could. And he did it because he just thought he could get away with it. And I was not going to let him get away with it. I mean, like all the men in my life I've let hurt me. And that was my belief back then, that I was the victim."

The board covered a lot of the same ground as the previous board, but they also seemed more interested in her progress and growth while in prison.

Deputy Commissioner Gardner:

"Do you think that if we were to release you, you would fail? Because we release lots of people and usually, falling back into alcohol or drugs is why they get brought back in."

Inmate Mathews:

"I'm well aware of my addictions. I have no need to test the waters any further with them."

Deputy Commissioner Gardner:

"Anything in particular with all this voluminous self-help that you've done that you're particularly proud of?"

Inmate Mathews:

"AA. I love AA. My 'Aware Class.' We created a victim awareness class. And that was after the Battered Women's Investigation. I think that helped me take better accountability. I was able to share that stuff with others. And it was a great class. It was based on restorative justice."

The Commissioners seemed to be leaning in the direction of release when they began to question Cheri about how she might fare on the outside, when abstaining from alcohol would be a condition of parole.

Deputy Commissioner Gardner asked Cheri to imagine what might happen if she were offered a drink that had been spiked with alcohol. And she took a big swig of rum and coke.

"They spiked the drink and you didn't know, but now you've violated your condition of parole. And then the question is – a week later – the parole officer says, 'Hey, how's life?' Would you share that with him?"

Inmate Mathews:

"Would I share that with him?"

Deputy Commissioner Gardner:

"He's never going to know. They're not going to know. And it was only a little and it wasn't your fault."

Inmate Mathews:

"Well, I believe that – I haven't taken a drink in 15 years. So taking a drink is something that's important. I'd admit in AA or anywhere else whether it's an accident or not. And I would not have a problem being honest with my parole officer. So if somebody slipped some rum in the drink, I'd be honest, tell my sponsor, go to a meeting and continue on with my life.

Deputy Commissioner Gardner:

"What if you got a jerk parole officer and this guy might actually lock you back up? Would you tell him?"

Inmate Mathews:

"Wow. I don't know. I think I would just let him know and tell him what I did about it. I would rather just be upfront and honest with my parole officer than try to start hiding things. Because I think that would be ridiculous."

As fate would have it, Cheri would face almost this exact scenario a couple of years later, when she was starting a new life in Colorado. She had a "slip," and drank a small amount of alcohol. And she volunteered that information herself, telling her parole officer, David King, all about it. Fortunately, King was not a jerk. In fact, he told me, "I have nothing but respect for Cheri. When she told me about this slip, she said, 'Dave, I screwed up.' And I said 'You just can't do that, Cheri.' And that was the end of it."

The parole board at CIW was interested in how someone like Cheri, who presented as such a capable, responsible person, could have been so deeply immersed in the world of drugs and addiction for so long. This was her response:

"I was addicted to sugar at a very young age. I was stealing candy. I was stealing money to buy candy. I was already in that addictive behavior. I moved from that to cigarettes. I went through constant punishment for smoking and continued to smoke regardless. So my addictive behaviors were already beginning before I ever started drugs. I believe I was looking for some kind of connection with people around me, taking me out of my feelings. I was terrified of my dad. Drugs numbed me. They made me feel better. My self-esteem was pretty much rock bottom my whole life. My dad emotionally abused me, and the drugs took that away. It took that feeling of inadequacy and like I was stupid and ugly and I would never amount to anything. I was abandoned by my mom when I was three and felt, in some way, that that was my fault, that my mother didn't love me. My dad stressed that she didn't love me or my sister, so that was another feeling of there was something wrong with me. There was something wrong when your mother doesn't love you. And drugs were a really great escape from that."

Judy: So, at the end of this hearing, did you feel more optimistic?

Cheri: Not at all. When we got out of the room and sat outside waiting for a decision, my lawyer said, "You know you're not getting out, right?" I said, "I know. I don't even know why I am here." We sat outside for 20 minutes, then they called us back in. They gave me a date for release. I went numb, just froze. So did my lawyer. He could not believe it had just happened.

Cheri was too numb to cry when the commissioners read the release statement.

They noted the unusual number of laudatory letters written by corrections officers, program leaders, other inmates, and more.

From the official transcript:

Deputy Commissioner Gardner:

"You've been nothing but a model inmate. And there's nothing that we could see that would lead us to believe that you're currently an unreasonable risk to public safety. Just the opposite. The Commissioner and I certainly feel comfortable in releasing you. I don't think you're a threat to public safety."

They praised Cheri for her honesty in admitting that she had killed Frank Belize, even when her attorneys, over the years, had told her not to talk about that crime.

"You admitted doing it. And we weren't here to try that case. But clearly, we were impressed that you've admitted that over many years, even talking to the police as recently as 2010 about that."

And then, they outlined the conditions of her parole: abstaining from alcohol and drugs, submitting to regular testing. Lifetime parole, in California, allows for a review of the case every five years. In the meantime, the parolee has to obtain permission as to where to live and work and be subject to regular visits from a parole officer.

Cheri: I went back to my cell. I was numb. I kept thinking they would take it back. The governor can overturn it, after all. He can do that right up to the date you're supposed to be released.

Not much chance of that. Jerry Brown was on the record saying that "if the individual is eligible for parole and the board determines they are no longer a threat, the law says they must be paroled." And beyond those legal strictures, Brown had also been quoted about his core belief that people can change, as a factor in granting parole: "I have been brought up in the Holy Roman Catholic Apostolic Church, and redemption is at the very core of that religion."

Redemption. As Cheri knows all too well, it's a lifelong process.

Chapter 34

"No More Walking In Circles"

In the movies, when an inmate is finally released from prison, there is often an emotional scene in which the newly-freed prisoner is finally reunited with his or her family. But that's in the movies. In Cheri's case, she had told her kids about her release date, along with the information that she would be spending six months in a recovery house in Beaumont, California, before she would be allowed to move to Colorado to be with them. A stranger came to meet her.

Cheri: Somebody picked me up at Chino to take me to Beaumont. He was driving a Prius, I think. I had not been in a regular car in so long, riding in the front seat, with a seatbelt on! Or in any vehicle, really, without shackles, in regular clothes. He drove first to a Quik Mart and asked if I wanted to go in and get something. But it was too much for me, so I just stayed in the car while he got me a soda. I was overwhelmed, just kept thinking, "I'm not in prison, I'm not in prison," emotionally stuck on that thought. I have no memory of what we talked about. It was a short ride to Beaumont.

It was October 3rd, 2014, 16 years after she was sentenced to prison. The outpouring of emotional well-wishes from her friends – inside and out of prison – was enormous. From Facebook posts

("Cheri Mathews is coming home! Praise God") to personal letters from old "bunkaroos," like Claudia Chita, who had been released years earlier:

"Cheri!!! I cried! And cried!!! Then I was overwhelmed by all the '1sts' you get to do. What crazes are you gonna really dig, like 'Organic Food,' 'Fake Eyelashes,' all the new cars! Most of all, I have this overwhelming feeling that another piece of my heart is free.

Cheri, I am so extremely happy for you, but happier for me because I get my friend back with no walls. Maybe there is a high school track we can walk together and solve the world's woes. I am a dork, I know. No more walking in circles, ha, ha, just long paths to who knows where. Yay! I can't wait until we are a text message away from each other!

Love, Claudia"

Of course, "text message" was not yet a familiar phrase to Cheri.

Cheri: Yeah, the "firsts." My first trip to Walmart, yikes! It was overwhelming. I had a panic attack. After a half hour, I had to get out of there.

Judy: If it's any comfort, a lot of us feel the same way about Walmart.

Cheri: But cell phones, that was the big one. I didn't understand how they worked and couldn't have one, anyway, until I'd been in Beaumont awhile.

"Dearest Palma,

I got out October 3rd and am in this program until my transfer goes through to Colorado. I am so very grateful to finally be free. It is amazing. Of course, I'm restricted here, but it doesn't compare! Next month, I'll be allowed to get a job and a phone. Send me your numbers so I can call you. Have a Merry Christmas and Happy New Year, my friend.

Love, Cheri"

The residents at the halfway house were allowed to go out together to attend NA and AA meetings, but otherwise, she was regarded as an ex-con in a treatment center and closely monitored. And she was the only "lifer" in the group.

Cheri: That was my first adjustment. I had been a drug and alcohol counselor in prison, sober for 15 years. Now I was a participant in a drug treatment program. And I was not trusted. The first time we went to see a parole officer, in a van with other girls in the program, they called my name and said, "You have a hold on you, another charge." What? I hit the wall. Was it the other murder? I almost fainted. The room was spinning. Was I being sent back? Then I met with the parole officer, and he said, never mind, it was someone else. I went outside and lit up a cigarette. That's when I started smoking again. I felt so powerless. I had been considered trustworthy, but now I'm a 'convict.' And convicts are known for playing a lot of games.

And yet, Cheri was chosen by the counselors to get a job within a month of arriving, an honor usually bestowed no sooner than three months into treatment.

Cheri: They made an exception for me. I was a 'bus boy' at Grandma's Country Kitchen. The lady who owned it was amazing. It was a big, busy restaurant and I worked my ass off, keeping up with the tables. She ran a tight ship and hired excellent waitresses. They would share their tips with me because I would clean their tables so quickly. I had $1300 saved by the time I left.

Judy: How did you get to work?

Cheri: At first, I took the bus.

Judy: Another bus ride!

Cheri: It was strange. No shackles on, no mesh on the windows, normal people sitting beside me. The first time I rode on it was so profound I started sobbing on the bus. "Oh my God, I'm here!" It was a profound moment of freedom.

Judy: I'll bet.

Cheri: But eventually I got a bike to ride to work. I wanted to stay in shape. And it felt so free, riding by myself, under my own power.

Cheri had a couple of visitors while she was in the halfway house. Casey Lain and Ray Harrison had known (and adored) Cheri since the 90's, when they were all involved in the crazy world of meth. Now, both men were clean and sober, working at good jobs. Both had written to Cheri in prison, and were eager to see her again. Casey was the first to show up.

"She had changed," Casey told me, "because she was *sober*. But she was still Cheri. She still had that aura -beautiful, tall, stunning, a glow about her. It was a cool visit. I asked if she'd like to go to Starbucks and she said, 'What's a Starbucks?'"

Ray visited her next.

Cheri: Ray wrote me a lot in prison. He drew the funniest pictures, little stick men acting out scenes, little hearts on everything. We were all really close. They are like little brothers to me.

"I wrote her the whole 16 years," Ray told me. "The whole time. Holidays, sending her photos and money. I loved her and cared for her. She came out a God-fearing, loving woman. It was a transformation. No addictions. No drama. When I went to visit her (in Beaumont), she still looked like Cheri. Beautiful. Those eyes. As if 16 years had not gone by. We hugged and talked. She leaned back in her chair and said, 'So, what's up?' Just like she always did."

Cheri was 38 years old when she went to prison. She got out at 53. As far as her friends were concerned, she was as vibrant and fun as ever, but also better. They all were. Sober and sane. And lucky to be alive, one day at a time.

And there were plenty of days ahead of her, a new life waiting in Colorado with her kids and grandkids. Her transfer from California was approved a month ahead of time, short of the usual requirement of 6 months in a treatment facility.

Cheri: The day after my transfer came through, Michelle and Jason were there to pick me up. I felt so much joy! Oh my gosh, I felt loved and forgiven. I mean, they came together to get me! The two most important people in my life. They brought Jasper, my only grandson. I met him for the first time.

"After she was paroled, Michelle and I decided to drive there and get her," Jason told me. "It was like a surreal dream. I hoped that, at last, I would have a relationship with my Mom. She was always on our minds, but I was horrible about writing her in prison. I was angry and didn't want to have anything to do with her. But she really worked on herself in prison. Now I am really proud of her."

"How was the drive home to Colorado?"

"It was a dreamlike state. Surreal. We didn't talk too much on the drive. I did give her a big hug, I remember. She looked really good."

Cheri: I remember the drive to Colorado. They let me drive! I had taken the written test to get my California license renewed, so it was legal. It was a huge part of feeling free, to drive a car again. And we spent the night in a motel. Amazing. When we arrived in their town of Nucla, I was given the upstairs bedroom in Michelle and Vince's house.

Judy: And so began what's known as "lifetime parole."

Cheri: Right. Free, and yet, not.

Chapter 35

Life After Life

Nucla is a town of some 700 souls in Southwest Colorado, nestled atop a lush mesa and dotted with family farms and orchards. Although Nucla is surrounded by high desert plateaus, it owes its fertile green meadows and orchards to a ditch that brings water up 350 feet from the nearby San Miguel River, a ditch engineered by a socialist commune in 1894. The fact that the community was settled by socialists is somewhat ironic, given the right-wing political bent of those living there today. Trump banners abound (still) and the local governing body made national news a few years back when it passed an ordinance requiring everyone in town to own a gun, an ordinance that was not enforced but was nevertheless quite popular with the residents. Nucla boasts a lovely town park, a single main street of on-again-off-again businesses, including the Apothecary and the 5th Avenue Grill, where Cheri and I first met over lunch.

Cheri wasn't sure what to expect from her new home, at first, but she wasted little time settling in. She sent out a Christmas letter that first year to all her friends, describing her new life:

Merry Christmas Everyone!

I am sitting at the library typing this as I have yet to get a computer of my own, and since I had carpal tunnel surgery it hurts like hell to write. So I apologize for my negligence in staying in contact. I am living my dream. I mourned my loss of mothering my children during my incarceration, and now I have 5 grandchildren to make a living amends to my children by being a grandmother to them. My family is amazing, exhausting and hilarious. There are no dull moments!

I have a minimum wage parttime job at the only grocery store in town (pop. 700). This enables me to babysit my 3 year old granddaughter Cambree and my 9 month old grandson Jasper for my daughter and son-in-law, whom I live with. My son Jason and his wife Shannon live 10 doors down with my other 3 granddaughters — Jayde (8), Emma (4), and Abby (1). She is a stay-home mom or I would probably be ready for a breakdown. All 5 at once is a bit overwhelming.

Besides work and babysitting, I finally went skydiving in Utah with my daughter Michelle! OMG it was amazing!!! Can't wait to take my son this summer. The country is beautiful and the wildlife is flourishing. Most people hunt here. I have lived off of deer, elk and bear meat since I arrived. Much better than I thought it would be. I dated a super nice guy for a minute, but he had control issues and wanted a full-time wife. I am not ready for that much commitment so I had to cut him loose.

For the ladies in prison --never, never give up. You know I never really believed I would be released. I was obviously wrong. For the ladies in the program, sit your asses down, listen, learn, and take advantage of what the program offers. For the ladies in the free world, congratulations and happiness. For my crazy, beautiful family, I would not trade you in for any gift on earth. I love you all,

Cheri

Of course, as we all know, Christmas letters don't always tell the whole story. The past six years have had more than enough challenges.

Cheri's first job — at Redd's Mercantile — proved to be a good way to get to know the locals.

Cheri: I really liked it. I got to meet everyone in town during the three years I worked there. People were coming in to see who I was. They had heard I had killed someone.

Judy: Did that bother you?

Cheri: No. It was natural curiosity. Mostly women. They would sometimes say stuff like, "I'm sure he deserved it." Once that was over, the curiosity, it was fine. And everyone knew and liked Michelle, which helped.

Her parole officer, David King, convinced the Colorado Department of Corrections to pay for Cheri to go to truck driving school, a move he believed would help her case when it came time to appeal to the California authorities for release from lifetime parole. She completed that course (no surprise there) and started driving for a local company.

Cheri: I started driving for Williams Construction, but I soon realized "I'm too old for this!" It was hard, physical work, up and down out of the truck, lifting things, shoveling snow off the equipment. I have six screws in my foot from bunion surgery in prison, when they had to break my foot and then straighten it again. The up and down of 12 hour days, at 15 dollars an hour, it got to me.

"It wasn't always easy for Cheri," her parole officer told me. "There were a couple of blow ups with her family, not always smooth sailing. But I never worried about her. I look at it like this: 'Would I want her to be my neighbor?' And my answer is, and always was, 'Yes, absolutely.' It was an honor to work with her."

Those first five years of serving lifetime parole in Nucla definitely had their ups and downs. Cheri worked a variety of jobs, from waitressing (where I first met her) to establishing her own cleaning service, with high-end clients in Telluride. That, too, was hard physical work, since she cleaned huge homes alone or with just the help of one other person, often her son Jason. The "ups" were those moments with her kids and grandkids, when she got a glimpse of what a sober, free life could mean. She told me once about an idyllic day she had just spent with her family, at a Father's Day barbecue in 2020, down by the Dolores River . "At one point," she said, "I realized I was swimming in this beautiful river, in this beautiful place, surrounded by all five grandchildren. It was a 'moment,' as they say. Everything I had ever hoped for."

But the "downs" became more and more frequent. Her sister Susie showed up, and moved in with Cheri, into the home Cheri was renting and fixing up. Susie was on meth, which would have constituted a parole violation for Cheri if it had been known she was housing a known drug user with a felony record.

Cheri: I thought I had forgiven her, but I hadn't. It came down to a confrontation to throw her out. It was really hard, but I did it.

I spoke briefly with Susie Shaw over the phone about this eviction by her sister. "I was mad and hurt when she asked me to move out," she told me, adding, " but that's all behind us now. I love my big sister. Cheri has always been my protector, my lifeline."

Susie had a long track record of dividing the family and disrupting their lives. Michelle, who has worked hard to maintain her sobriety and resented her aunt for introducing her to drugs when she was young, made it clear she did not want Susie anywhere near her or her children. Jason was more forgiving, although he, too, had resentments.

"Susie was passing the dope pipe to me when I was 13 years old. Back then, I hated her for starting me on meth. I blamed all my problems on her. But not now. I understand addiction better, and I see how she became who she was from living with a father who didn't love her. She is very childlike. I love my Aunt Susie." Susie has since moved back to Fallon, Nevada.

Jason has waged his own battle with addictions, including drugs and gambling. He and his wife have divorced, but he often visits her and his kids in Fallon, Nevada. "Gambling is my worst addiction," he told me, "and that's why I live in Colorado. I can't be in Nevada."

Then, in mid-Covid, 2021, Michelle's husband was offered a good job in New York State supervising a large-scale farming operation. They were given free housing and the children were enrolled in an excellent school. It was an opportunity they could not turn down.

And just like that, Cheri was alone. "My bubble had burst," she said. All the grandkids had moved away, and she felt lonely for the first time since she was released from prison.

On the plus side, she finally won her freedom.

"I heard from the California Department of Corrections four months AFTER they had made the decision," her parole officer told me. "I immediately called Cheri and said, 'How much do you love me?'"

"I was with her when she got that call," Jason told me. "We were cleaning a house in Telluride. We laughed and were so happy."

Long pause.

"Then you wait for the next storm. That's how it happens for us. But when it comes to my mother, I know, I KNOW she's going to be good. She has changed the world for people around her. Takes a certain person to come off a meth addiction, to overcome the abuse she suffered, to come out the way she is now."

"I'm very grateful to have her back in my life. I never had that nurturing as a kid. And now I do."

Once Cheri was completely free, off "lifetime parole," she was also free to travel, without first asking permission from California authorities. So she and her friend Susan Rice, the librarian in Naturita who had become a close friend, flew to New York, visited Michelle and family on Long Island, saw the sights in the city, even took a carriage ride through Central Park. There were a lot of "firsts" for Cheri, including the security lines at the airport. "They took all my toiletries," she complained, "because no one warned me that you can't carry this stuff on the plane."

But this was a journey to celebrate, far removed from those old days of "taking a geographic," when she ricocheted between meth and murder and motherhood.

CHAPTER 36

"What Do You Think NOW?"

As Cheri and I approached the end of our collaboration in piecing together her story, an intense journey for both of us that lasted more than a year, I asked her if she would consider writing a letter to her late father, expressing those feelings she had never had a chance to express when he was alive. She wrote that letter, but it was not at all what I had expected. Expectations, of course, are tricky things. I had hoped she would tell him off, express anger at the way he had emotionally and physically abused her, anger at the "code" that made it so difficult to ever ask for help, much less believe she ever deserved it.

But that would have been *my* take, not hers. And her take comes from a place of hard-earned compassion, from years and years of self-reflection and honesty and amends, from understanding at a very deep level that the only way to deal with "the wreckage of the past" is to let go of all the blame and toxic resentments.

So here it is, just as she wrote it:

Hey Dad,

It has been over 37 years since I last said goodbye to you, and I still miss you so much. I thought we would have more time to grow up together, to share our pain and happiness, to actually learn to commu-nicate, but shit happens and it happened to you at 42 years old. Life is so fucking unpredictable. I certainly did not expect to lose you, Penny, Kevin, Ronnie and Mom — all so young. I believe you have always been a constant companion of my soul through all I have experienced, ever watching me through all my madness. Of course, I have no idea if that is true or not, but your voice has spoken to me in my darkest moments, and I have managed against all odds to survive it all. So has Susie, and that in itself is no small miracle since the both of us have been crazy our whole lives. So here I am at 60 years old, ready to have that conversation with you.

As they say, "Better late than never."

Since I believe you are with me now, you already know Judy is writing a book about my life. She begins with your question, "What do you think?" Hah! Remember that one? I had no idea what to say to you and it would piss you off every time. I wish I could have found out exactly what you were trying to get out of me, but to this day, I haven't a clue. I can, however, share what I think about it all today. Not just what I think, but what I choose to believe about the events of my life.

My beliefs through my life created my reality. It is a hard thing to say goodbye to old ways of thinking. No matter the chaos they created in my life, they were familiar and comfortable. They were what you taught me, and all I knew was what you raised me to believe was the truth. But the real truth was that I lived a lie for well over half of my life.

So let me tell you what I think about my childhood today. I have no desire to rehash the past, as that is what this book is about, but I believe I understand so much more about you as I have walked many miles in your shoes. In the 60s and 70s, there were rules society lived by. There was never a mention of mental illness, addiction, family dynamics, or the abuse suffered by these afflictions. "What happens in the home stays in the home," we believed. I didn't share our family "business" for many, many years. The world has changed, thanks to the men, women, and children who had the courage to share their experiences.

Judy believes that mine will help someone, somewhere. I truly hope so.

Today, I understand the obsession you had with mom. You never got over her leaving us, you spoke of her with a hatred that didn't make any sense at the time, but does now. You had obsessive, compulsive thinking. You never understood that forgiveness sets **you** free, not the person you forgive. Uncle Raymond had it [obsessive-compulsive thinking], I have it and your grandson Randy has it. It is a real disorder and so destructive for us and for those around us. I never realized I suffered from it because it was my "normal" way of thinking. That is, until I had already killed two men and served more than 10 years on my life sentence.

Raymond died in prison the same year I began my life sentence. Randy is also facing a life sentence, and I can only hope and pray that he will seek help this time.

When I found myself plotting a murder sober, I realized there was something very wrong with me. I couldn't blame meth this time. I sought psychiatric help and have been on medication ever since. I cannot express the gratitude for the peace a simple pill has given me through the years. I still get angry, but I know my anger is a secondary emotion to some other initiating feeling, usually fear or embarrassment or hurt. I can now address the primary emotion and find forgiveness for myself and for others in order to resolve it.

You were hurt, angry and full of fear. You didn't know better, so you projected that on Susie and me. I believe with all my heart that when you know better, you do better. You never had the chance to know better, and I bitterly regret that. I forgave you a long time ago, water under the bridge that was swept away by years of growing insight.

So now, the question: Did the horse come before the cart? You taught me how to survive a violent world, and I did. But did I create that violent world or was it already there? I believe it was both. The meth world is sick and violent, the twilight zone of this modern age. "Normal" people cannot understand, but meth heads can. It's like the wild west in hyperdrive. Never a dull moment while your life goes nowhere. But hell, it goes nowhere FAST. I loved it because I fit right in. I had zero self-esteem, an upbringing that taught me to be tough no matter what I faced, and a deep, underlying fear that I could never be good enough. Meth took some of those away and amplified others. I had no fear of death, so I created life-and-death situations. Every time I survived, it became clear to me that I was protected no matter what happened. I didn't know why and I didn't care. I became delusional and invincible.

Everything you taught me led me to decisions that ended lives and saved mine. That world was there long before I showed up on the scene, but since then I have watched Susie, Mandy, Randy, Michelle and Jason live in that same world and survive it without killing. The difference between me and them is YOU. I became you on meth. I don't know whether to thank you or kick your ass. If those situations had transpired anyway, I would not be writing to you, I would be with you right now. So I choose to thank you. I do not think of myself as invincible anymore, and life is way too short to hold grudges.

As it is, your legacy and Mom's legacy live on in us. Mom was bi-polar in the extreme. An absolutely amazing woman by any standard. Beautiful, talented and smart. She was an exceptional horse trainer and rider, she was gifted with the arts of leather work, silver work, ceramics, and cooking. She raised big cats! Anything she set her mind to, she accomplished. That was when she was up.

When she was down, her time was spent in institutions, gambling, divorces, and finally suicide. I respected her decision to end her life, but I miss her so much. She pulled some shit on me, but was there for me through thick and thin, as she was for everyone. You two must have been quite the pair. Fire and Fire. Susie takes after Mom. She is Mom on meth.

Your daughter Mandy takes more after her mother [Penny], gods be praised. She is stronger than me or Susie, lost you at 11 and Penny at 16, has raised Cameo and Irish pretty much on her own, lost her husband, lost her inheritance (with my help), works hard and moves forward. I miss her and hope she knows how proud I am of her and how much I love her. I know you do.

You were able to meet your first grandson, Randy, and your first granddaughter, Michelle. Since then, you are blessed with two more grandsons, Jason and Blake. They are all amazing, smart and talented. They are also challenged with that addictive gene that plagues us all. You have 9 great-grandchildren to date: Jayde, Emma, Cambree, Abigail, Jasper, Lawrence, Elisha, Amirah and Zedekiah. May they have the good fortune to grow and prosper, knowing they are accepted and loved unconditionally.

So, what do I think? I think that acceptance is the key to change and, subsequently, peace. I had to accept the truth of who I was. I was fear-based, and terrified of anyone knowing. I developed an ego that sought to protect me by attacking anything that threatened to expose me for what I truly was: a coward. I took the coward's way out, time and time again. Drugs, divorce, leaving my children, prostitution, gambling, running away. Always running, but wherever I ran, there I was. Finally, murder. I think I killed Davey to escape the madness that had engulfed me. The final chickenshit move. I was the very definition of a loser.

The miracle of that realization was that it set me free. The truth really does set you free!

How fucking amazing is that? I could now move forward knowing I never had to be that person again. It took me many years in prison, many wonderful women who helped me through it, and the love and support of friends and family. It does take a village to raise a child and I am grateful to be finally growing up.

Have I arrived? Hell, no, and never will. It's all about the journey.

I will see you soon, Dad.

Your loving daughter,

Cheri

Chapter 37

Take Two:
Cunning, Baffling And Powerful

"If you want to make God laugh, tell him your plans." That's an old saw, I know, but I seem to have a hard time learning the lesson.

I had planned to end this story with Cheri's letter to her father. But reality kneecapped my writer's hubris, the hubris that led me to believe that I could shape the outcome of someone else's story, that I could shape the arc of this tale by bending it towards a happily-ever-after redemption.

Alcohol had other ideas.

Just as I was closing in on the end of the book, after more than a year of conversations with Cheri, conversations with all those friends and family who enriched her story with their own perspectives, with all those deep dives into parole board transcripts and court hearings, Cheri came over for lunch to talk about the wrap-up.

Sitting at my kitchen table, she lobbed a grenade into the conversation.

"I need to be honest with you. I have decided to start drinking, just some beer at my home in the evenings, because I don't think it's a problem."

And just like that, I was reminded of the power of addiction. And the power of old childhood messages. I was gobsmacked.

"Well," I responded with as much equanimity as I could summon, "You realize this changes things. It's no longer a story of redemption. Now, it's a story of seduction, about the siren call of addiction, that 'cunning, baffling and powerful' shit we both wrestle with every day."

I was angry, but mostly at myself, a sober alcoholic who should have known better than to think I could plan the arc of another woman's journey. But I was also upset. Upset with my failure to see the toll this project had taken on Cheri. Dredging up the details of her past, a deep dive unlike anything she had done before, had packed an emotional wallop. She confided that she had been fighting depression. Depression is a close companion to a slip.

Because she is my friend, because I love her humor and strength and compassion, I knew I would have to drop our project if that's what she needed to do. But in that tense moment in my kitchen, I wasn't ready to give up.

"Look at your body language right now," I said to her. Normally open and vibrant and energetic, Cheri sat in a chair across from me, leaning back with her arms and legs crossed, her body folded up in a defensive posture. "I can't help but wonder if this is the old Cheri," I said, "the Cheri who is an expert in self-sabotage. You know, the 17 year old girl frozen on the starting block at the swim meet, throwing the race because deep down she didn't believe she deserved to win. Think about it," I added. "You decide to start drinking just as we are about to finish and publish the book? Is that a coincidence?"

When she left that day, I wasn't sure I could finish writing. On the one hand, I was so very sad, because I feared she could not come back from this cliff. On the other hand, I was forced – once again – to understand that there is no "happily ever after" with addiction. Alcoholics talk about "one day at a time" for a reason. Staying sober for 24 hours seems achievable. Staying sober forever is a discouraging prospect. So the happy endings come in smaller bites, when we tuck into bed each night, feeling gratitude that our day was spent as a sober, conscious, helpful and caring person, rather than as an asshole who had spent the day wreaking havoc, disappointing those we love, and burning bridges.

On this occasion, Cheri stepped back from the cliff. A few days later, she told me she had stopped drinking again, not long after we had talked. In retrospect, I don't think it was an accident that she decided to tell me about her choice to drink again. She knew what my reaction would be and I think she wanted to hear it. And it was a sobering week for me, in other ways. I was reminded, in the most gut-wrenching way, that fantasizing some version of "happy ending" is a dangerous fiction for addicts and alcoholics.

So this is what I know, today, as I write this sentence: Cheri is clean and sober. She is committed, one day at a time, to staying that way. She is working on getting credentialed as a drug and alcohol counselor in Colorado, just as she was in California. The need is enormous; meth addiction is a plague in our rural community. Her qualifications, obviously, are superb. She speaks the language and knows the culture.

And now, I want to give Cheri the last word. This passage is from a letter she recently wrote to her nephew Randy (Susie's son), who is in prison, serving a life sentence.

What I want to tell you is that as long as you are breathing, it is never too late. Let me be that inspiration that proves it to you. They told me there was no chance for me, that I would never see freedom. What they did not know was that I was already free long before they cut me loose. Freedom, true freedom, isn't a place, but a state of mind. I made a decision to find out who I truly was and I found out I was a good person, a good teacher, a good speaker, and that I could use my experiences as a tool to help others. I see that you are also capable of that. But first you must realize that humility and truth are strengths, not weakness. Violence, prejudice, and living by the "code" are weak-ass bullshit. Have the courage to find and express who you truly are no matter what anyone else thinks or says. I found that I earned more respect for that than anything else. It was an amazing journey for me and I wouldn't, couldn't, trade it for anything, because it saved my soul. No regrets, no guilt. The past is perfect, because you cannot change one moment of it. It is what it is, and regretting it is a waste of time. You can, however, have remorse. We live, we learn, we change, we grow. Hopefully.

So with that I'll let you go. Know that you are loved, you always have been. But true love doesn't feed into bullshit, and true love is also a love and acceptance of self. I love you, but will not endanger my well-being and safety if you or Susie are not flying right. I hope you understand and respect that. Doesn't mean I love you any less, only that I love me today, too, and won't put myself at risk.

Love,

Aunt Cheri

"I love me today."
Finally, an answer to "What do you think?

December, 2021: Cheri traveled to New York to visit daughter Michelle and her grandchildren. This marked the first time she had traveled out of state, alone, without needing permission from a parole officer. It was also the first time she had seen a Broadway play.

ACKNOWLEDGEMENTS

I am deeply grateful to all those people who agreed to be interviewed for this book, including Cheri's friends from her prison days - Palma Kuykendall Paxton, Susan Mellon, Cerise Laberge, Claudia Chita, Charlotte Key and Penny Greer.

Cheri's family members were extremely gracious with their time, agreeing to share some very difficult memories. So we send a special note of gratitude to Jerry and Becky Mathews, children Michelle and Jason, sisters Susie and Mandy, and stepfather Ron Mori.

Crystal "Kit" Carson not only agreed to an interview, but also sent us numerous letters and documents that she had saved about Cheri. Casey Lain and Ray Harrison were invaluable in providing details of Cheri's outlaw life in the California desert.

Former corrections counselor Silvia Hedlind was most helpful in describing Cheri's rehabilitation in prison, and Montrose District Parole Officer David King filled in the blanks for me concerning Cheri's years of serving "lifetime parole" in Colorado. The California Department of Corrections, upon my request, promptly provided transcripts of both parole hearings, which were invaluable for telling that crucial part of Cheri's journey.

I want to thank my brother, John Mansfield, for alerting me to the possibility of a "good story" after he met Cheri waitressing in our home town of Norwood, Colorado.

Cheri's own writings and her vivid recollections, along with her astonishing honesty throughout our time together, are the heart and soul of this book. I am honored to have been entrusted with her story.

Last, but never least, my loving gratitude to my partner George Lewis, who served as my primary editor on this project. He was also my cheerleader, encouraging me to keep going, even when the going got a bit rough.

ABOUT THE AUTHOR

Judy Muller is an award-winning broadcast journalist, author, and professor emerita of broadcast journalism at USC's Annenberg School of Communication and Journalism.

Before coming to USC, Muller was a correspondent for ABC Network News, reporting for such broadcasts as *Nightline, World News Tonight with Peter Jennings, Good Morning America, 20/20 and This Week.* During her 15 years at ABC, she covered such stories as the Rodney King beating trial and subsequent riots, the Presidential campaigns of Paul Tsongas and Bob Kerrey, the L.A. earthquake in 1994, the O.J. Simpson case and numerous environmental stories throughout the West. Prior to joining ABC News, Muller spent nine years as a correspondent for CBS News, where she was a contributor to *CBS Sunday Morning* and *CBS Weekend News* on the TV side and as a commentator and reporter on the radio side. She covered the space shuttle program, both national political conventions in 1988 and the 1988 George Bush presidential campaign. Muller was previously an anchor/reporter for KHOW in Denver and WHWH in Princeton.

During her career, she has won numerous Emmy awards for her reporting, two Edward R. Murrow awards, two Columbia-DuPont awards, and a Peabody Award in 2010 for an investigative series on marijuana dispensaries in Los Angeles (for public television). She has been a contributing commentator for NPR, and a contributing correspondent for Al Jazeera America and PBS' News Hour. She has written many articles about flyfishing, her passion, for *Sports Illustrated* and other fishing publications.

She is the author of two other books: *Now This: Radio, Television and the Real World,* (Putnam, 2000) and *Emus Loose in Egnar: Big Stories from Small Towns,* (University of Nebraska Press, 2006). She makes her home in Norwood, Colorado.